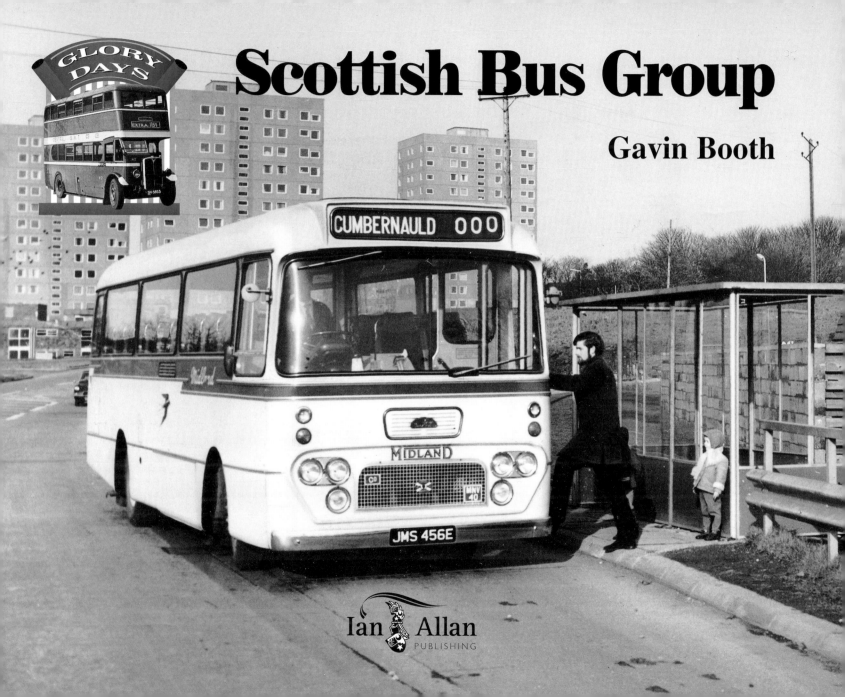

GLORY DAYS

Scottish Bus Group

Gavin Booth

Ian Allan
PUBLISHING

Contents

Introduction	3
1. The Rise of the SMT Group	5
2. State Ownership	13
3. The SBG Companies	19
4. Under Scottish Transport Group Control	27
5. The SBG Fleet	81
6. The SBG Legacy	95
Further Reading	95

First published 2000

ISBN 0 7110 2710 2

All rights reserved. No part of this book may be reproduced or transmitted in any form or by any means, electronic or mechanical, including photocopying, recording or by any information storage and retrieval system, without permission from the Publisher in writing.

© Ian Allan Publishing Ltd 2000

Published by Ian Allan Publishing

an imprint of Ian Allan Publishing Ltd, Terminal House, Shepperton, Surrey TW17 8AS.

Printed by Ian Allan Printing Ltd, Riverdene Business Park, Hersham, Surrey KT12 4RG.

Code: 0004/B2

Introduction

This book completes the trilogy of titles dealing with the three main company bus groups in Britain since World War 2. The earlier titles, *Glory Days: BET Group* and *Glory Days: Tilling Group* covered the story of these groups to the formation of National Bus Company in 1969. In the case of Scottish Bus Group, there was no significant change to the company at that time, so this covers the period from its sale to the state, in 1949, through to the major reorganisation in 1985 that anticipated the even greater changes ahead — deregulation and privatisation. Arguably these were SBG's glory days — from the heady days of the postwar travel boom through to the increasing uncertainties of the 1980s, when economic and political pressures did so much to dent the morale of the British bus industry before it rose to the challenge and regrouped in its present form.

Scottish Bus Group was very different from its counterparts in England and Wales. It did things its own way, and earned a reputation for careful financial housekeeping and conservative vehicle purchases.

For me, SBG was different from Tilling and BET because I worked for the group for 26 years and saw much of what is reflected in this book at first-hand. I was fortunate enough to meet many of the great characters who moulded SBG, and work with many talented bus people.

Although organised as a group, the companies had a tremendous degree of autonomy, and the Alexanders way of doing something was very different from, say, the Western way. This individuality has attracted enthusiasts over the years, and was reflected most obviously in the buses and coaches the companies purchased. There was some influence from head office, of course — often a requirement to buy a proportion of the group's intake from Bristol/ECW, or Leyland, or Alexander Coachbuilders. But how the companies interpreted this created much interest.

There was some interchange of ideas between SBG and NBC, partly because the managing directors sat on each other's boards, but there was widespread relief in Scotland when SBG chose not to travel the corporate identity route with its buses, settling instead for a corporate livery for its London coaches, followed by the Scottish Citylink identity for its express operations. The buses continued to wear their own distinctive colours right to the end, admittedly with standard fleetname styles from 1978.

Gavin Booth
Edinburgh

3

A famous photograph, but an important one that records the birth of the Scottish Motor Traction and, later, Scottish Bus groups. Although SMT had operated experimental services in West Lothian late in 1905, Maudslay 52 (S 543), with 34-seat body, seen here at the Mound, Edinburgh, on 1 January 1906, is generally regarded as the first SMT bus, and certainly started regular services. SMT bought 16 Maudslays in 1906-9, and there is photographic evidence that the double-deck bodies could be swapped for charabanc bodies.
Gavin Booth collection

1. The Rise of the SMT Group

Right from the start, the men who moulded what was to become the SMT group, and ultimately the Scottish Bus Group (SBG), believed in motorbuses. Unlike the Tilling Group with its roots in horsebuses, and the BET Group with its involvement in electric tramcars, the pioneers who were working to establish services in various parts of Scotland recognised the potential of the motorbus from an early stage and, although trams play a small part in the group's history, SMT was more interested in persuading municipalities to abandon their trams in favour of buses.

Three father-and-son dynasties dominate the story of the development of the SMT group — the Alexanders, the Dicks and the Swords — but it is important to remember that the SMT company was set up right at the dawn of the motorbus era by a man who left his mark on the industry right to the point of nationalisation: William J. Thomson. Although the Thomson family played no more part in the business, it was William's foresight that laid the foundations for much of

Scotland's bus industry. With others he set up the Scottish Motor Traction Company (SMT) in 1905 and, after experiments in West Lothian, started a double-deck service on 1 January 1906 between the centre of Edinburgh and Corstorphine, now a city suburb but then beyond the city boundaries and the reach of the Edinburgh tramways.

The SMT company grew, operating first into Midlothian and West Lothian, and after World War 1 into East Lothian. Its early expansion was largely organic, but in the 1920s SMT embarked on a substantial acquisition programme, most notably into the Scottish Borders with the purchase of Brook & Amos of Galashiels in 1926, although a less obvious acquisition that gives a clue to SMT's ambition was Dundee Mechanical Transport Co, operating well away from SMT's southeast Scotland base. SMT's Dundee area spread into Angus, and remained an isolated outpost until 1949 when the services were sensibly transferred to the Alexanders company.

While SMT was expanding in the east of Scotland, Walter

Further west, Walter Alexander was starting to build his business, and this photograph shows Walter at the wheel of his second bus, a 1916 Scottish-built Belhaven charabanc, 2 (MS 1723). This vehicle could be converted for goods-carrying work during the week; it appears to have been withdrawn by 1919. *Gavin Booth collection*

5

Western SMT's main predecessor, BET's Scottish General Transport Co Ltd, bought 12 of these Leyland SG7 buses with 40-seat bodies in 1924, Nos 51-62 (SD 8151-62). The Scottish Transport fleetname anticipated the creation of the Scottish Transport Group more than 45 years later. *Gavin Booth collection*

Alexander was developing a bus business based in Camelon, Falkirk, but gradually stretching to Stirling, Glasgow, Edinburgh, Perth and Dundee. As with SMT, initial growth was slow. When W. Alexander & Sons Ltd was incorporated in May 1924 there were little more than 20 vehicles in the fleet, but growth in the later part of the 1920s was more dramatic; fleetnumbers had reached over 200 by 1930.

Another strand of what would become the SMT group was Glasgow General Omnibus & Motor Services Ltd (GOC). Set up in 1926, GOC, which initially had associations with the London General company, operated from Glasgow into Lanarkshire, and invested heavily in new buses. In 1928 it became associated with SMT, but in 1930 the London, Midland & Scottish Railway company (LMS) bought GOC's assets. The LMS also bought two other sizeable Lanarkshire operators in 1930 — Stewart & McDonald of Carluke and J. W. & R. Torrance of Hamilton; GOC absorbed these businesses in 1932.

The only part of what became the SMT group with a tramway background was the Scottish General Transport Co, set up by the British Electric Traction Co (BET) to bring together its various Scottish interests. It had three tramway companies: Airdrie & Coatbridge, Greenock & Port Glasgow, and Rothesay. Trading as Scottish Transport, it controlled all these interests, tramway systems and feeder bus services; the Airdrie & Coatbridge trams passed to the local authorities in 1920, but Scottish Transport held on to the bus services.

Meanwhile, there were important developments at SMT. A 'new' Scottish Motor Traction company was set up in 1929, effectively acquiring the 1905 company, but with the LMS and LNER (London & North Eastern) railway companies jointly owning half of the new SMT. The four main-line railway companies, alarmed by the spread of motorbuses in the 1920s, had agitated for bus-operating powers, but largely chose to exercise these powers by investing in emerging bus companies. SMT was chosen as the vehicle for most railway interests in Scotland, and the LMS and LNER were the only two of the 'big four' operating in Scotland.

Things now started to happen, with the help of the railway money. In 1929 SMT acquired a controlling interest in W. Alexander & Sons, making the SMT company the principal bus operator over much of eastern and central Scotland. Its first

main foray into southwest Scotland came with the acquisition of John Sword's Airdrie-based Midland Bus Services. This substantial company had local and long-distance (including Glasgow-London) services. Midland was operating into the area served by the Scottish General Transport Co, and some rationalisation seemed desirable. The agreement between SMT and the railway companies prevented railway investment in BET's Scottish Transport subsidiary, so in 1931 BET sold it to SMT. Scottish Transport assumed control of Midland in 1932,

shortly before Scottish Transport was renamed Western SMT Co Ltd.

At around the same time, the enlarged GOC companies, already under LMS control, passed to SMT to become Central SMT Co Ltd. From these recently-acquired companies came the other families that dominated SMT for so many years. John Sword of Midland Bus Services was put in charge of the new Western SMT company, and R. B. Dick of Stewart & McDonald ran Central SMT. Their sons would continue the

The Bluebird name will always be associated with Alexanders, and was first coined for its touring and long-distance coaches in 1934. The first Bluebird coach was a rebodied 1929 Leyland Tiger TS1, but also in 1934 there followed 30 Leyland Lion LT5Bs with 32-seat Alexander coach bodies, including P157 (WG 2361). The sliding roof and roof-mounted luggage rack will be noted, as will the chrome steps leading to the rack. This coach carries the original style of Bluebird logo, which was soon replaced by the more familiar style that appears on several vehicles illustrated in this book.
Gavin Booth collection

family connection well into SBG days, as Walter Alexander Jnr followed his father at the former family business. William Thomson, as SMT Group Chairman, recognised that these shrewd, canny Scots had built successful businesses in the unregulated and highly-competitive 1920s, and their down-to-earth management skills would be an asset to the new SMT empire, particularly following the 1930 Road Traffic Act which brought order out of some of the previous chaos, and introduced legislation and regulation to control the fast-growing bus industry. SMT had been suddenly propelled into the role of a major territorial bus group, rather as Tilling and BET, separately and jointly, found themselves in England and Wales.

Outside the four main Scottish cities — Aberdeen, Dundee, Edinburgh and Glasgow — which had their fiercely-protected tram/bus operations, SMT's services covered most of central and southern Scotland, with the Alexanders empire stretching north to Fife, and north of the Tay to Aberdeen and the north east.

There were parts of Scotland where SMT's influence was weaker, and sometimes non-existent. In the south west, the Caledonian Omnibus Company had been set up in 1927, and

by 1928 was under the control of the Tilling & BAT group; after the 1942 reorganisation, Caledonian became a Tilling group company — the only one in Scotland. Caledonian worked jointly with SMT companies on trunk routes, but had a network of local routes in the Solway coastal strip between Carlisle, Dumfries and Stranraer.

SMT had no involvement in local services in the Highlands & Islands area. David MacBrayne was the main operator of trunk and local services in the West Highlands, and the area around and to the north of Inverness was in the hands of the Highland Transport Co, set up by the LMS railway to take over the Inverness & District company. MacBrayne's and Highland Transport were exceptions to the rule that SMT would manage the railway interests in Scotland. The LMS and Coast Lines owned MacBrayne's, and the LMS had a half-share in Highland Transport. SMT presumably had its hands full developing its business in Scotland's more populous areas, but (as we shall see) the MacBrayne's and Highland Transport companies would eventually come under the control of SMT and its successors.

The new SMT company set out on a process of organic growth and acquisition in the 1930s, in much the same way

that the Stagecoach empire grew from a Scottish base half a century later. The four group companies — SMT, Alexanders, Central SMT and Western SMT — eliminated much of their competition during the 1930s; in some cases SMT group buses replaced tramways.

SMT's operations extended from Berwick-upon-Tweed through the eastern Borders to Edinburgh and the Lothians, with some slightly anomalous operations based on Airdrie, just to the east of Glasgow, and the isolated Dundee outpost. An official definition of the SMT area, published in 1947, describes it as 'the territory south of the Forth and east of a line Bo'ness-Glasgow-Biggar-Carlisle'. Many of the company's acquisitions in the 1930s were coach operators, building up its position as a major provider of day and extended tours. However, its most significant purchase in the 1930s was probably the bus operation of BET's Musselburgh & District (Coast Line) company in 1937; until 1928 the company had operated trams, but had turned to buses to compete with other operators.

Alexanders covered the largest area, stretching from Falkirk and Glasgow to the north east, described in 1947 as 'north of a line Bo'ness-Glasgow-Helensburgh', which a glance at any map reveals as a vast part of Scotland. In practice its services covered central Scotland, Fife, Perth to Inverness and everything east of that.

Not all of Alexanders' acquisitions were absorbed into the parent company. Pitlochry Motor Services and Simpson's & Forrester's were formed in 1929, the latter combining two Fife businesses. The most significant expansion of the Alexanders business came with SMT's purchase in 1930 of the Scottish General group of companies, operating in an area similar to Alexanders' and with companies like the General Motor Carrying (GMC) company in Fife, and Scottish General (Northern) in Elgin, which both fitted well into Alexanders' portfolio. GMC continued as a separate operation until 1937.

Alexanders then proceeded to mop up the tramway systems in its area — the Kirkcaldy trams were replaced by Alexanders' buses in 1931; the Perth Corporation trams had been withdrawn in 1929, but Alexanders acquired the municipal buses in 1934. The Perth and Kirkcaldy urban buses carried a dark red livery until the 1960s. Falkirk and Dunfermline trams were replaced by Alexanders' buses in 1936 and 1937. A red livery was also used for the buses of David Lawson Ltd. This Kirkintilloch operator was taken over in

Western SMT adopted this striking white/black livery in 1934, and these continued to be the colours for Western's coach fleet long after the buses, from 1945, appeared in red/cream. Photographed in Lancashire before delivery to Kilmarnock is CS 7021, a 1938 Leyland Titan TD5 with 56-seat highbridge Leyland body. No fleetnumbers were carried on Western buses at this time; in the 1949 numbering scheme, this bus became 122. It was withdrawn in 1956.
Gavin Booth collection

During World War 2, Central was one of many operators to loan buses to London Transport, allegedly to cover shortages but possibly as much to do with maintaining national morale. M2 (SN 5853), a 1933 AEC Regent 661 with 52-seat Cowieson body, had joined the Central fleet in 1936 with the business of Baillie Bros, Dumbarton. It is seen in Trafalgar Square, London, in December 1941.
London Transport

1936 and remained as an apparently separate operation until 1961.

Another separate operation was Lanarkshire Traction, taken over by SMT in 1932 and placed under Central SMT control, although outwardly it functioned as a separate company. This gave Central virtual domination of Lanarkshire. The 1947 definition is 'an area bordered by the line Glasgow-Biggar-Muirkirk-Glasgow', though it adds that the company 'now also operates the narrow but populous strip running west from Glasgow along the North Bank of the Clyde to Dumbarton, Helensburgh, Alexandria and Balloch'. This area came in 1936 with the Baillie Bros and Clydebank Motors businesses, although acquisitions by Central SMT were always rare.

Western SMT grew steadily in the 1930s. From 1932 SMT agreed to provide bus services to replace Ayr Corporation trams, and these were managed by Western. The same year, SMT took over Kilmarnock Corporation's bus services. These gave Western two important urban networks to complement the many trunk and longer-distance services it was developing. The Western area, in the 1947 definition, was 'south of the Clyde and west of a line Glasgow-Muirkirk-Dumfries-Carlisle'.

By the end of the 1930s the SMT group was a power in the land, operating nearly 3,000 buses and coaches. Like all transport operators, it sometimes struggled to cope with the demands of World War 2, but as a mature and well-organised company, it was well-placed to deal with these difficulties. Massive fleet investment in the 1930s, replacing a mixture of

types inherited from its constituent companies with sturdy vehicles, many diesel-engined, helped the group to come through the war in fairly good shape.

SMT was not just a bus company. It had successful car and commercial vehicle dealerships, and became involved in commercial aviation. During the war it used its engineering and construction skills to build Duple-design utility single-deck bus bodies on Bedford OWB chassis, as well as tank landing-craft, at its Marine Gardens premises at Portobello. It was also involved in bus bodybuilding through Alexanders, which had built bodies for its own use for many years, but as part of the SMT group increased its output to become a major supplier to the group. During the war, Alexanders rebodied many late prewar single-deck chassis with new utility-style double-deck bodies to give much-needed extra capacity.

The SMT Group, 50%-owned by the LMS and LNER, found itself in the brave new postwar world facing the possibility of voluntary or compulsory state control. The 1945 Labour Government had declared its intention to nationalise the railways and long-distance haulage, and floated the possibility of compulsory nationalisation of bus services under

area schemes. The railway shareholdings in Britain's territorial bus companies passed to the new British Transport Commission (BTC) in 1948, and there was pressure on Tilling, BET and SMT to sell their privately-held stakes. Tilling sold out first, in 1948, and SMT followed in March 1949, though the sale was backdated to April 1948. The purchase price for the SMT group was £26.8 million. BET mounted a vigorous anti-nationalisation campaign and held out in private ownership.

SMT now found itself part of the new BTC, but in practice day-to-day control continued much as it had done before. Sir William Thomson — he had been knighted following a term as Lord Provost of Edinburgh — retired in 1949, and died shortly afterwards. His successor, now Chairman of the newly-titled Scottish Omnibuses Ltd (SOL), was James Amos, previously SMT's Traffic Manager and a pioneering Borders busman who had come to SMT with the Brook & Amos business in 1926.

The rest of the SMT company was not acquired by the BTC, and the non-bus interests remained in private hands. SMT's bus interests were transferred to the new company Scottish Omnibuses Ltd, although 'SMT' remained as a fleetname on the Edinburgh company's buses for several years, as well as forming a part of the Central and Western names. Scottish Omnibuses was also the group's parent company, sharing office accommodation at New Street, Edinburgh, with the SOL bus company. On 15 May 1961, Scottish Omnibuses Group (Holdings) Ltd was formed, to separate group from company functions, and, following the end of the BTC and its replacement by the Transport Holding Co (THC), the holding company name was changed to Scottish Bus Group Ltd.

SMT resumed its Edinburgh-London services after World War 2 with Duple-bodied AEC Regals like B239 (ESC 433), seen arriving at St Andrew Square, Edinburgh, when new in 1946. *AEC*

2. State Ownership

The new state-owned Scottish group wasted little time in widening its sphere of influence and sorting out some existing anomalies.

At Western there was some substantial tidying-up. The company had separate subsidiaries as a result of 1930s acquisitions — Greenock Motor Services and Rothesay Tramways — and these companies were absorbed by Western in November 1949. Western had also bought W. & R. Dunlop of Greenock in 1945, and maintained this as a separate entity; this too was merged with Western in 1949. Tilling's Caledonian company had passed to the BTC in 1948, and it made sense to wind up the company and pass it to the Scottish group in December 1949; most services passed to Western. In March

1949 the BTC bought Young's Bus Service of Paisley and its associate, Paisley & District, and these too passed to Western control, being fully absorbed by the end of 1950. All these acquisitions increased the size of the Western fleet by more than 400 buses, pushing the fleet total towards 1,000.

The vast Alexanders company grew with the overdue transfer of the former SMT Dundee area services, and the 1947 purchase of the Greig, Inverness, business; this was followed three years later by the takeover of the bus services of Sutherland of Peterhead. 1950 also saw the acquisition of Wemyss of Ardersier, although this part of Alexanders' territory was relinquished to the new Highland Omnibuses company in 1952. One part of the Alexanders empire that

13

Acquisitions swelled the Western fleet in 1949-51, including the business of Young's, Paisley, taken over in 1951. A mix of Albion, Bedford, Daimler, Guy, Leyland and Maudslay vehicles joined the Western fleet. This is one of 13 Maudslay Marathon III coaches, two of which had Scottish Aviation 33-seat bodies like Johnstone-based JM2200 (XS 6983), new in 1950, which lasted with Western until 1960.
Gavin Booth collection

remained in the hands of the family was the Stirling-based coachbuilding concern; this became Walter Alexander & Co (Coachbuilders) Ltd, but remained a major supplier to SBG for the rest of the group's history; at the same time, Alexander Coachbuilders was actively looking for non-SBG work to allow it to expand, and it enjoyed some success with municipal fleets and ultimately with the BET Group.

By comparison, the early state-owned years were quiet for SOL and Central. As we have seen, SOL lost its Dundee area to Alexanders, and gained the former Caledonian Dumfries-Edinburgh services. Central absorbed Lanarkshire Traction in November 1949.

One further consequence of railway nationalisation was the creation of a fifth major Scottish group company. The 50% holding in Highland Transport held by the LMS automatically passed to the BTC, and the balance followed; the BTC then passed the management of Highland Transport to Scottish Omnibuses and, having also acquired the bus services of Macrae & Dick, transferred that firm's licences to Highland Transport. A new company, Highland Omnibuses Ltd, was set up in February 1952 to combine these businesses, and to take over Alexanders' isolated Inverness outpost. Initially, the new Highland company adopted SOL procedures, and SOL kept a fatherly eye on this new addition, which beyond the Inverness area had inherited some of the most underpopulated parts of

Scotland, and which would rely heavily on the profits the Scottish group made in the central belt for its survival. Highland also relied on the more prosperous companies for cascaded vehicles, tempered by a modest investment in new buses and coaches.

The group now consisted of five main companies — Alexanders, Central, Highland, Scottish Omnibuses and Western — and this would remain the group structure until 1961.

The pioneering families were still very much in charge of their companies. John Sword, R. B. Dick and Walter Alexander were on the group board along with their sons William Sword, R. B. Dick Jnr and Walter Alexander Jnr; the fathers had stepped down from day-to-day responsibility, and the sons were now general managers of the former family businesses — but one can visualise the constant presence of the fathers at their sons' shoulders. Only Scottish Omnibuses and Highland were free of any family involvement.

Although under overall BTC control, the Scottish group continued in its own way. The BTC, it seems, had more than enough worries over British Railways and, to a lesser degree, London Transport, to worry about the Tilling and Scottish groups — particularly as they continued to turn in respectable profits that helped offset some railway losses and improve the BTC's overall performance.

Scottish company general managers had a significant level of autonomy from the group. While the management structure was common — general manager, traffic manager, chief engineer, company secretary — and the company structure broadly the same — with district traffic superintendents in charge of local depots (always 'depots' in Scottish parlance) supported by depot engineers, inspectors, foremen and platform, office and maintenance staff — each company had its own distinctive way of doing things, and there was never any real danger that central control would impose uniformity on everything that the companies did. This, in many ways, was part of the appeal of the SBG way of doing things.

As we shall see, the companies also enjoyed a certain amount of autonomy in their vehicle purchases, and the Scottish group differed from the Tilling group and London Transport in that it regularly bought from state-owned Bristol and Eastern Coach Works (ECW), but also bought at least equal numbers of types available on the open market. This may have had something to do with capacity at Bristol and ECW,

14

but the indications are that the Scots were keen to keep their options open (and perhaps also to support Alexander Coachbuilders), and resisted any move to buy more than just a proportion of Bristol/ECW products. However, while Bristol single-deckers never gained universal acceptance in Scotland, the Lodekka was bought in respectable numbers for many years.

Figures for the 15 years under BTC control show the Scottish group's revenue growing steadily — from £9million in 1948 to £23.1million in 1962. Over the same period, total working expenses rose from £7.4million to £20.5million. The group was consistently profitable, and Central SMT was the star performer. Working into industrial Lanarkshire without any of the 'glamorous' operations like extended tours and long-distance services to get in the way, Central's 1956 net profit, for example, was £964,767 — an impressive 42% of the Scottish group's profits that year, and an amazing 22% of the combined Scottish and Tilling profits. The group's profits over this 15-year period must be set against fluctuating passenger numbers, which rose from 547million in 1948 to 825million in 1955, but then started a slow but steady decline to 735m in 1962.

The sheer size of the Alexander company led the Scottish group to carry out a significant restructuring in May 1961. From 15 May that year Alexanders was split into three, with new companies created — W. Alexander & Sons (Fife) Ltd, W. Alexander & Sons (Midland) Ltd, and W. Alexander & Sons (Northern) Ltd. Alexanders had previously operated in three divisions, so the new companies largely continued operating over familiar territory, but with senior management appointed where previously everything was dealt with through Falkirk.

Alexander (Midland) reflected the genesis of the empire, operating in central Scotland, with important networks of services in Falkirk, Stirling, and around Glasgow, and as far north as Perth. Its head office was at the traditional W. Alexander address of Brown Street, Camelon, Falkirk. When new liveries were adopted for the new companies in 1962, Midland stuck with Alexanders blue.

Alexander (Fife) had as its fairly well-defined and self-contained operating area the Kingdom of Fife, with substantial urban operations in Dunfermline and Kirkcaldy. The company head office was at Esplanade, Kirkcaldy.

Alexander (Northern) inherited a large area, from Dundee

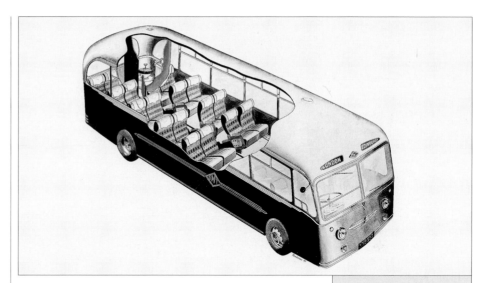

and Angus north to Aberdeen and along the Moray Firth coast into Inverness. The company head office was initially at its depot at Gairn Terrace, Aberdeen, but moved to the bus station at Guild Street.

At the same time as Alexanders was split, the former W. Alexander company was renamed Scottish Omnibuses Group (Holdings) Ltd, a recognition of the need for a distinct holding company. In September 1963 this company was renamed Scottish Bus Group Ltd. The same year the Scottish group appointed a new Chairman, only its second. When James Amos, an old-school pioneering busman, retired he was succeeded by Moris Little, whose impressive bus industry career had previously been in the municipal sector. When appointed to SBG, Moris Little was Transport Manager at Edinburgh Corporation and, a few years later, when SBG became master of its own destiny, he was well qualified to steer a successful path dealing with transport professionals and politicians, both in Edinburgh and in London.

The long-standing Alexanders subsidiary company, David Lawson Ltd, ceased trading on 1 January 1961, and in March 1962 was renamed Clydeside Omnibuses Ltd, a move which seemed to presage a split of the large Western SMT territory, possibly in conjunction with discussions that were underway for SBG to take over Glasgow's Corporation buses. Nothing

▲ The group's flagship Scotland-London services had been operated by specially-designed coaches since the 1930s, many with toilet accommodation and ultra-luxurious seating. The services restarted after World War 2 with more basic vehicles, but the competition from Northern Roadways of Glasgow led to the building of 40 of these very early (deliveries started in April 1951) AEC Regal IV coaches, which were divided between Scottish Omnibuses and Western SMT. This cutaway illustration of the Alexander bodywork shows the 30 Chapman reclining seats and the toilet compartment at the nearside rear. *Gavin Booth collection*

15

Scottish Omnibuses had a London office at 298 Regent Street, where SOL's B465 (KSC 542) a 1953 AEC Regal IV 9822E with 38-seat Alexander body, is seen being passed by London Transport RT2828. The two-day London service indicated on the Regal's blinds was a sightseeing service that ran between Edinburgh and London, and vice-versa, visiting tourist centres en route. There were east coast and west coast variations, as well as three- and four-day equivalents. *Gavin Booth collection*

SBG had an ongoing programme of building basic, functional depots for its companies. This is Western's Cumnock (C) depot, opened in 1954, with work in progress on (from left): Y1033 (GYL 391), a 1945 ex-London Transport Guy Arab II/Northern Counties; GA299 (BAG 98), a 1946 AEC Regal O662/ Burlingham; and CL607 (CSD 13), a 1949 Leyland Tiger PS1/Alexander. *Gavin Booth collection*

came of the Glasgow talks, and even the formation of a separate company to manage the group's operations in Renfrewshire and along the Clyde coast came to nothing at that time — though the idea, and part of the name, would resurface more than 20 years later.

Scottish Omnibuses Ltd, which had continued to use the SMT diamond as a fleet logo, had moved on to the fleetname 'Scottish', but in 1964 adopted the more geographically accurate 'Eastern Scottish'.

There were still bus companies outside the Scottish group operating in Scotland. Most notable was David MacBrayne, with just over 100 buses in 1952. The LMS railway company had held 50% of the shares in MacBrayne since 1929, and this holding passed to the BTC in 1948. MacBrayne was principally a shipping company, so it would not have made sense to transfer management to SMT, as happened with most of the railway holdings in bus companies in the southern part of Scotland.

MacBrayne aside, the best-known independent bus companies in Scotland were grouped around the Glasgow conurbation, in Ayrshire, or scattered around Scotland's northeast corner. The acquisitive SMT group had eliminated much of the potential competition in the 1930s, and the BTC had made some sensible purchases in the late 1940s. There were still smaller independents, often in rural areas, which were tolerated because they covered routes that the Scottish group would have found difficult to serve economically. The more sizeable independents were a nuisance, but the group managed to mop some of them up.

In 1958 the Glasgow independent, Lowland Motorways, was bought by Scottish Omnibuses, bringing an amazing selection of vehicles and services in Glasgow's east end. Three years later Central bought Laurie of Hamilton, which traded as Chieftain, with a mostly double-deck fleet and services in Hamilton and the growing new town of East Kilbride. One of the best-known independents, Baxter's of Airdrie, sold out to

Scottish Omnibuses in 1962, strengthening the company's Airdrie outpost. In 1964 SOL bought Stark's of Dunbar, with which it had enjoyed a close relationship for over 30 years.

Four well-known independents in Alexander (Northern) territory were taken over in the 1960s — Strachan of Ballater in 1965, Simpson's of Rosehearty in 1966, and Burnett's of Mintlaw and Mitchell of Luthermuir in 1967. Alexander (Midland) acquired Carmichael of Glenboig, trading as Highland, in 1966, gaining better access to another of Scotland's new towns, Cumbernauld.

The railway closures that followed the Beeching Report in 1963 involved SBG in a great deal of planning to provide replacement bus services, and over the years group companies were required to provide replacement services for unremunerative railway lines.

SBG continued to battle against rising costs and falling passenger numbers through the rest of the 1960s, but major changes were on the way which would affect the state-owned companies as well as the largest municipal bus operations.

The BET Group had remained out of state control, although the BTC held roughly half the shares in BET's bus companies through the main-line railways' investments in the late 1920s and early 1930s. BET, always a profit-driven organisation, was moving quickly away from reliance on its bus companies to produce the level of return it sought, and was diversifying into many new types of business, all over the world. For BET, the last straw was the announcement of proposals for Passenger Transport Executives (PTEs), which were to be created in some of the very conurbations that were most profitable for BET, notably Birmingham, Manchester and Tyneside. In 1967 BET agreed to sell its shareholdings in its UK bus companies to the Transport Holding Company, and this paved the way for a new super bus group in England and Wales. The new National Bus Company (NBC) controlled both Tilling's and BET's bus companies — in essence, everything in England and Wales outside the municipal/PTE orbit.

These changes signalled the end of THC, and brought control of Scotland's company buses back into Scotland. A new body, the Scottish Transport Group (STG), commenced operations on 1 January 1969 — the same day as NBC.

SBG also built bus stations and, in cases like this, combined depot/bus stations. This is Scottish Omnibuses' Kelso (E) depot, with three AEC single-deckers — B338 (FFS 235), a 1948 Regal III O682 with a 1953 Scottish Omnibuses body; B385 (GSF 704), a 1949 Regal III with a 1954 Burlingham Seagull body; and B799 (USC 799), a 1960 AEC Reliance 2MU3RV with Alexander body.
Gavin Booth collection

SBG had two depots in England, at Berwick-upon-Tweed and Carlisle. Western's Lonsdale Street depot in Carlisle had been built in 1938 by Caledonian, but passed to Western with that company in 1950, although it was treated as a sub-depot of Dumfries until 1977 when it got its own depot code (E). Two Western Bristols, DT1597 (OCS 719), a 1960 MW6G with 41-seat Alexander body, and B1630 (RAG 396), a 1961 LD6G, bound for Glasgow and Gretna respectively, sit outside the depot. Between 1957 and 1962 Western bought a total of 70 LS6Gs and MW6Gs with Alexander 41-seat bodies — the only LSs and MWs built for any customer which did not carry ECW bodywork; although Alexanders bought LSs and SOL bought LSs and MWs, these all had ECW bodies. *Gavin Booth collection*

The 1961 division of Alexanders into three companies had least obvious effect on the new Midland fleet, which retained the traditional Alexanders blue livery, but with new fleetnames as worn here by MRA12 (AMS 12), a 1948 Leyland Titan PD1 with Alexander 53-seat lowbridge body to the style which combined Leyland and utility features. It is seen in 1965 in the rather stark surroundings of Cumbernauld town centre, running on a town service. It was withdrawn in 1967. *Gavin Booth*

18

3. The SBG Companies

In 1949, when the state-owned Scottish group was set up, there were four main group companies. Here we look at these companies and their territories, and then at the new Highland company.

Scottish Omnibuses Ltd

In 1949 the group's parent company, based in Edinburgh, had depots at Airdrie, Bathgate, Berwick, Broxburn, Dalkeith, Galashiels, Hawick, Kelso, Linlithgow, Musselburgh, Peebles and Selkirk. At that time it also had depots in Blairgowrie, Dundee and Forfar for its isolated Dundee outpost. The company head office was at New Street, Edinburgh, where it would remain until privatisation.

Always one of the most high-profile group companies,

SOL's buses provided essential transport for mineworkers in Midlothian and millworkers in the Borders, as well as commuters into Edinburgh and Glasgow. As Edinburgh grew in importance as a tourist destination, the company developed a sizeable touring programme and a network of long-distance services. SOL's services to the East Lothian coast and into the Borders were well used for leisure travel.

Until 1949 SMT buses had carried a blue/cream livery, but with the formation of Scottish Omnibuses a light green/cream scheme was adopted. From the mid-1960s a darker green, Lothian Green, replaced the light green. In SBG liveries, the word 'cream' is open to a wide interpretation. For some companies the relief colour was almost white, for some off-white, and for some — notably Western — a rich cream.

The two main acquisitions by Scottish Omnibuses in the 1960s, Baxter's of Airdrie and Stark's of Dunbar, resulted in these company names being retained and mainstream SOL vehicles appearing in less familiar liveries. The Stark's takeover was an interesting one: under a long-standing agreement, Stark's had operated the Dunbar-Edinburgh route using buses carrying SMT/SOL fleetnames, as well as local services in East Lothian which were labelled 'Stark's'. After the takeover the buses based at the former Stark's depots at Dunbar and North Berwick (both coded S) all carried Stark's names, and further buses were drafted in to this fleet. B672S (SWS 672) was one of four AEC Reliance 2MU3RV models with 38-seat Alexander bodywork transferred from the main SOL fleet in 1964, and is seen in St Andrew Square, Edinburgh, in the light green/cream applied to the Stark's fleet. It was one of 20 'two-day' Reliance coaches bought in 1959 which carried this unique style of Alexander body.
Gavin Booth

When SOL took over Baxter's of Airdrie in 1962 it started painting the acquired buses in green/cream, but local opposition led to a reinstatement of the Baxter's blue/ivory colours; these were later applied to buses transferred from the main fleet, like AA893V (YWS 893), a 1962 Bristol FLF6G with ECW 70-seat body, transferred to Baxter's Victoria (V) garage in 1963 and additionally carrying the Baxter's fleetnumber 93. The 'B' in the number blind reflects the prominent 'B' carried by Baxter's own buses. *Harry Hay*

Painting and varnishing could change the appearance of what were basically similar colours; Central and Western, for example, used essentially the same livery, but the Western version always looked richer and brighter.

SOL's main service network was based on Edinburgh. High-frequency services operated out of the city to the Musselburgh and Dalkeith areas, fanning out from Musselburgh towards North Berwick, Haddington and Dunbar, and from Dalkeith to the small mining towns of the Midlothian coalfield. Longer-distance services to the east and south of Edinburgh ran to Berwick-upon-Tweed and on to Newcastle (hourly, jointly with United — a 5hr 25min journey), and there were other, less frequent Edinburgh-Newcastle services via Jedburgh and Kelso.

Most towns and villages in the Borders had some form of bus service, though some were very infrequent and only operated on market days. The main towns had regular links to Edinburgh, and there were town services in Berwick, Galashiels and Hawick. SOL also provided timetabled services

for workers at the woollen mills in Galashiels, Hawick and Selkirk. Directly south of Edinburgh were frequent services to Penicuik with an hourly service to Peebles and Galashiels.

West of Edinburgh, SOL ran three stopping services to Glasgow — the main route (every 15min) via Bathgate and Airdrie (journey time 2hr 13min) and the less frequent, slower services via Shotts or Bellshill. Like so many Scottish trunk routes, these services carried some end-to-end traffic, but provided a wide range of short-hop opportunities along the route. In the 1950s a limited-stop service between Edinburgh and Glasgow was overlaid on these.

SOL also had a substantial network of local services within West Lothian, town services in Bathgate, and its Airdrie-based routes into Glasgow. Services to Falkirk, Stirling and beyond were operated jointly with Alexanders.

The company operated a wide range of day, afternoon and extended tours, and a number of longer-distance services, most notably the Edinburgh-London route. In 1949 there was one year-round service to London, an overnight trip taking 15hr

19min, augmented in the summer by a daytime service. There were seasonal long-distance services from Edinburgh to Aberdeen and Inverness, and joint services (with Ribble) over the border to Blackpool, Liverpool and Manchester. There was also a summer service between Glasgow, Newcastle and Whitley Bay, joint with United.

As time passed, SOL expanded in the west with the acquisition of Lowland and Baxter's and following Glasgow Corporation's decision to abandon its tramways beyond the city boundaries, and in the developing new town of Livingston. When the Forth Road Bridge opened in 1964 the company started a number of joint services with Alexander (Fife) to Dunfermline and Kirkcaldy. New depots were opened at Baillieston, for east Glasgow services, and at the new town of Livingston.

W. Alexander & Sons Ltd

Before the 1961 split, Alexanders covered a huge swathe of Scotland. Looking at the 1949 situation, we start in what was

then known as the **Southern Area**, but would be dubbed Midland after the split. Depots in this area at various stages were at Alloa, Balfron, Bannockburn, Callander, Crieff, Kilsyth, Kirkintilloch (David Lawson Ltd), Larbert, Milngavie, Perth, Pitlochry, Stepps and Stirling.

The varied nature of this area meant that Alexanders was providing everything from rural services and longer trunk services to intensive urban services around Glasgow, some to the vast new housing schemes being developed in the postwar period. Alexanders also had a successful day and extended touring programme. Although year-round cross-border services were left to SOL and Western, Alexanders operated a network of longer-distance services within Scotland.

Alexanders' buses were traditionally azure blue/cream, and the Midland company retained these colours after the 1961 split. The buses of its subsidiary, David Lawson, were dark red/cream, as were the buses used on Perth city services. The Alexanders head office was at Brown Street, Camelon, Falkirk.

Starting in the company's heartland, around Falkirk, an

intensive network of services operated in and around the town, including the former tram route, the 10min-frequency Larbert Circular, and the high-frequency service linking Maddiston, Falkirk and Grangemouth. The most frequent services in the Stirling area were to Alloa (20min frequency) and Dunfermline (30min frequency, across the Kincardine Bridge). Overlaid on these were trunk services from Stirling and Falkirk to Edinburgh, joint with SOL, and to Glasgow (from Crieff/Callander via Stirling and from Bo'ness/Falkirk). Alexanders also had a network of services around Glasgow, principally to Milngavie.

Further north, there was a significant group of routes around Perth, notably the former Corporation town services, still branded in early state-owned days as Perth City Transport services, with buses in a dark red livery operating a range of high-frequency routes. There was also the nominally-separate Pitlochry Motor Services company, with routes centred on that

town. To the north west, Alexanders had its isolated Oban section, with a small selection of local services and a town service.

From Glasgow, Alexanders operated long-distance services to Aberdeen, Inverness and Oban, and trunk services to Dunfermline, Kirkcaldy, Leven and St Andrews.

The **Fife Area** had depots in Anstruther, Cowdenbeath, Cupar, Dunfermline (two garages until 1961), Kelty, Kirkcaldy, Methil (Aberhill), Newburgh, and St Andrews. A depot was subsequently built to serve the new town of Glenrothes.

With the concentration of industry and population in west Fife, many of the company's busiest services operated in this area. The services in east and north Fife were more rural in nature. The Fife coast was a popular holiday destination, particularly from Glasgow and the west of Scotland, and long-distance and coastal services satisfied this demand. The buses in Fife — apart from the dark red-painted Kirkcaldy town

23

The Northern Area buses were Alexanders azure blue/cream until 1962 when, following the split, the new Northern company adopted a striking yellow/cream.

The most frequent service in the area was the Culter-Dyce service, running through the centre of Aberdeen and providing an additional city service. The sparsely-populated nature of northeast Scotland meant that most of the other main services covered long distances, like the hourly services linking Aberdeen with Banff and Inverness (inland and via the coast). However, there were local services in and around Banff/Macduff, Elgin and Huntly, and in 1949 Alexanders still had a significant presence in Inverness, with a network of town services which would later pass to the new Highland Omnibuses company.

North of Aberdeen, Alexanders' presence would be strengthened with the acquisition of the Sutherland business, bringing trunk routes from Aberdeen to Peterhead and Fraserburgh, and the 1960s takeovers of Burnett's and Simpson's would augment operations in the northeast corner; the Strachan takeover would improve coverage on Deeside.

South of Aberdeen, in 1949 there were local services around Stonehaven, Montrose, the coastal Dundee-Carnoustie/Arbroath services and a Dundee-Inchture-Perth service. The transfer of SMT's Dundee area would give Alexanders a presence in Blairgowrie, Brechin, Forfar and Kirriemuir.

Central SMT Co Ltd

For many years the most profitable Scottish group company, Central operated in the compact Lanarkshire area and north of the Clyde to Dumbarton and beyond. It had depots in Carluke, East Kilbride, Hamilton (two depots), Harthill, Motherwell, Old Kilpatrick and Wishaw, while head office was at the old Lanarkshire Traction premises at Traction House, Motherwell. Central buses were red/cream, at one stage relieved by brown; a small fleet of Bedford and Albion private hire coaches was operated, painted blue.

Central's strength lay in intensive services around industrial Lanarkshire and into Glasgow. In 1949 it had no long-distance services as such and, while its depots provided local coach tours, this was a very small part of its business. It was very much a down-to-earth working bus company, with the times of many of its services designed to fit the shift patterns at pits and steelworks. Its one long trunk service operated hourly

Central's only big takeover in SBG days was of Laurie of Hamilton, which had bought the second Leyland Atlantean to operate in Scotland — XVA 444, a 1960 PDR1/1 with MCW 77-seat body. This became Central HR1 in 1961 and lasted there until 1969 when it was sold on to Graham's of Paisley. A second Atlantean was delivered to Laurie just before Central took over; this was sold on to A1, Ardrossan. HR1 is seen at the Carlton Terrace terminus, by the Clyde in Glasgow. *Harry Hay*

service buses — were azure blue/cream until the 1961 split when Ayres red was adopted.

Dunfermline operated a busy network of services, including town services and high-frequency services to Rosyth/ Inverkeithing, and to Lochgelly and Lochore/Ballingry. There were also the high-frequency Kirkcaldy town services, and frequent services between Kirkcaldy and Leslie and Lochgelly.

Cowdenbeath, Cupar, Leven and Lochgelly had locally-based services, and there were the long coastal services — Burntisland-Upper Largo, Leven-Newport — providing regular links along the Forth and Tay coasts.

The **Northern Area** ultimately had depots at Aberdeen, Alford, Arbroath, Ballater, Blairgowrie, Braemar, Buckie, Dundee, Elgin, Forfar, Fyvie, Huntly, Inverness, Lumphanan, Macduff, Montrose, Peterhead, Stonehaven, Strathdon and Tarland — though some of these housed only a few buses. A depot was opened in Fraserburgh in 1975.

Aberdeen was the natural trip attractor for the north east, and many services radiated out from the city. The long trunk services provided a variety of trip opportunities, linking villages with market towns.

between Glasgow, Lanark and Peebles, and this carried much of its leisure travel, as did services into the beautiful Clyde Valley.

The company's most frequent services ran into Glasgow from Carluke, Hamilton, Motherwell and Wishaw, with frequent services to slightly distant points like Airdrie, Shotts and Strathaven. These were augmented by local service networks in places like Coatbridge, Hamilton, Larkhall and Rutherglen.

The main Dumbartonshire area services were Glasgow-Balloch, Glasgow-Helensburgh, with more local services like the high-frequency Glasgow-Clydebank, Glasgow-Duntocher, and local services in Dumbarton. These would be challenged following the electrification of British Railways' north bank services in 1960, and the arrival of the 'blue trains' led to frequency and service cutbacks. This was partly offset by the remarkable growth of East Kilbride new town, which became a

very profitable traffic generator for the company at a time when traditional Lanarkshire industries were closing.

Western SMT Co Ltd

In 1949 Western had depots at Ardrossan, Ayr, Calderbank, Cumnock, Girvan, Gourock, Kilmarnock, Largs, Newton Mearns, Renfrew (Inchinnan) and Sanquhar, while its Greenock Motor Services and Rothesay Tramways subsidiaries had depots in these towns. There were also the services of W. & R. Dunlop of Greenock, taken over in 1945, and run as a separate entity until 1949. With the integration of the Caledonian services in 1950, Western gained depots at Annan, Carlisle, Dumfries, Kirkcudbright, Lockerbie, Longtown, Penpont, Wigtown and Stranraer, and the acquisition of Young's in 1950 brought depots at Johnstone and Paisley. The Newton Mearns depot was replaced in 1968 by a new depot at Thornliebank.

Western SMT replaced its Glasgow-London fleet more regularly than Scottish Omnibuses replaced its Edinburgh-London fleet. In the 1950s Western moved on from AEC Regal IVs to Guy Arab UFs and LUFs, and in 1960 bought 20 Leyland Leopard L1s — the first Leopards for an SBG company. They had Alexander 30-seat toilet-fitted bodies, and lasted until 1966, when they were replaced by 36ft-long Bristol RELH6Gs. Fifteen were sold to Ulster Transport Authority and the other five found homes in Scotland. Kilmarnock (K) depot handled the London services, and KL1606 (OCS 728) is seen loading at Victoria Coach Station, London, when new, with the tower of the BOAC terminal looming out of the mist in the background. These Leopards were reported to be achieving 16.89mpg at 50mph cruising speeds on the Glasgow-London service. *Leyland/Ian Allan Library*

25

Small buses hardly figured in SBG fleets in the 1960s, even in companies serving more remote rural areas. Highland bought eight of these Bedford VAS1s with Duple Midland 28-seat bodies in 1964, and went on to buy more VASs. CD1 (WST 500) is seen at the door of Thurso depot when new. It was withdrawn in 1977. *Gavin Booth*

The Western head office in 1949 was at its Portland Street bus station in Kilmarnock, though this moved to Nursery Avenue in the same town in 1961. Western's buses had carried a white/black livery from 1934, but from 1945 it adopted red/cream for its buses, staying with white/black for its coaches.

Covering a widespread area, Western had a structure of trunk services, supplemented by town services and other local routes. The main trunk route was the Glasgow-Kilmarnock-Ayr, running every 15min, and there was the less direct Glasgow-Paisley-Troon-Ayr service running every 30min. Other frequent services from Glasgow ran to Eaglesham, Mearnskirk and Neilston, and there were services to Greenock and Gourock, and on to Largs.

There were important Western service networks in and around Kilmarnock, including frequent services to Ardrossan, Ayr, Darvel, Irvine, Largs and Stewarton, and from Ayr to Airdrie, Annbank, Burnfoot, Dalmellington and Girvan, as well as town services. Ayrshire was still clearly the company's heartland in 1949, but imminent acquisitions would bring substantial new territory along the Solway coast (Caledonian) and around Renfrewshire (Young's).

Further afield, Western provided cross-border links from Glasgow to London (year-round overnight, summer daytime), and jointly with Ribble to Blackpool, Liverpool and Manchester.

Later company acquisitions included Clark of Dumfries and Murray of Stranraer, and in the Paisley area Western took over SCWS-owned Smith of Barrhead in 1968, and Cunningham of Paisley and Paton of Renfrew in 1979. Unlike other SBG companies, Western rarely took vehicles with its acquisitions, but the Paton takeover yielded 10 Leyland Leopards, some of which were sent to the company's Islay outpost.

Highland Omnibuses Ltd

This fifth major SBG company was added in 1952. Its vast territory included some of Scotland's least-populated areas and, although Highland regularly returned a modest profit, this was largely through good housekeeping, and a regular cascade of written-down buses from the profitable fleets in Scotland's central belt.

Highland had depots and outstations throughout its area. At various stages in its history, mainland depots were at Aviemore, Dingwall, Dornoch, Fortrose, Fort William, Grantown-on-Spey, Inverness, Kinlochleven, Nairn, Oban, Tain, Thurso and Wick; its main island depot was at Portree, Skye, but the David MacBrayne integration brought in depots at Tarbert on Harris, Port Ellen on Islay and Tobermory on Mull. Its head office was always in Inverness — first at Station Square, then at Farraline Park bus station, and later at Seafield Road.

Highland's livery was initially red/cream, but in 1970 it changed to poppy red/peacock blue, and then in 1980 the livery was simplified to poppy red/grey. From 1966 Highland's coaches were blue/grey.

Its most intensive services were around Inverness. There were the high-frequency Inverness town services as well as those radiating out from the town to Fort William to the south, Dingwall, Tain, Dornoch and Helmsdale to the north, and Nairn to the east.

There were small networks of services around Dingwall and Tain, and a virtually self-contained area in Caithness, around Thurso and Wick, including town services. The development of Aviemore as an all-year resort increased business in and to that town, while the MacBrayne business brought services on several islands and around Fort William, including town services.

Highland worked jointly with other SBG companies on services to the central belt.

26

4. Under Scottish Transport Group Control

For the first time since 1948 control of Scotland's company buses returned to Scotland following the formation of the Scottish Transport Group in 1969. This new body controlled not only the Scottish Bus Group, but also inherited the former British Rail-owned Caledonian Steam Packet Company as well as THC's half-share in David MacBrayne Ltd; the other half was bought from Coast Lines later in 1969.

The new STG initially had its headquarters at New Street, Edinburgh, shared with Scottish Omnibuses, but soon moved into a newly-built office, Carron House, in George Street,

Edinburgh. Moris Little remained as SBG Chairman and took up the parallel appointment of Deputy Chairman and Managing Director of STG. The STG Board consisted of Government appointees chosen from the great and good of Scotland, and included a part-time Chairman and the Managing Director of the National Bus Company (NBC); the STG Managing Director sat on the NBC Board.

At the birth of the new group, SBG consisted of seven bus-operating subsidiaries, a hotel, a public relations and publicity company, an insurance company, a travel agency and two

◄ SBG's notorious dissatisfaction with the Bristol VRT chassis led to their exchange for National Bus Company Lodekkas. Western KB2241 (NAG 592G), seen in Kilmarnock, was one of 39 VRTSL6Gs bought in 1969/70 with 75-seat ECW bodies. Thirty-six of these were withdrawn in 1973/4 and went to NBC fleets — 2241 went to Lincolnshire Road Car. The other three had already been withdrawn in 1972/3 and sold to a local dealer. *Gavin Booth*

27

Alexander (Northern) opened a new depot in Fraserburgh (FH) in 1975, and two new Ford R1014/Alexander Y-types are pictured at its opening. NT127 (KRS 127P) was a short-windowed 45-seat bus, and NT132 (KRS 132P) a 41-seat long-windowed (and twin-headlamped) coach. *Gavin Booth collection*

dormant companies. The bus companies were Scottish Omnibuses, Western SMT, Central SMT, Alexander (Midland), Alexander (Fife), Alexander (Northern) and Highland Omnibuses. The Garve Hotel had been acquired by SBG in 1964 and with it came bus services which were transferred to Highland. Scottish Omnibuses also owned a hotel — Dryburgh Abbey Hotel in the Borders.

The Travel Press & Publicity Company and SMT Insurance Company were long-established group subsidiaries; SMT Insurance was set up to handle all the group's insurance matters. The travel agency, Sanderson Travel, was a long-established Edinburgh company bought by the group and operated as a retail business.

The two dormant companies were Clydeside Omnibuses, mentioned previously, and Peter Burr (Omnibuses) Ltd, which had been set up following the acquisition of Peter Burr of Tongue in 1966, operating a mailbus service between Tongue and Thurso.

The seven bus companies accounted for £29 million of STG's 1969 turnover of £33.1 million There was a total fleet of 4,721 vehicles, operating 168.2 million miles and carrying 555.7 million passengers. The staff numbers totalled 17,843.

An early STG decision was that David MacBrayne's bus operations should cease and its services be split between other SBG companies. This process started in January 1970 and was completed by June 1972. Most of the northwest mainland services, as well as those on the islands of Harris, Islay, Mull and Skye, went to Highland, while Western took the Glasgow-Tarbert/Campbeltown services and the local services around Ardrishaig. Highland eventually withdrew from Harris, Islay and Mull as part of its policy to withdraw from more remote parts, leaving these services to local independents or Post Office mailbuses.

In 1973 the Greater Glasgow PTE was set up, and in 1975 local government reorganisation divided mainland Scotland into nine Regions, which were responsible for the co-ordination of road passenger transport services and the establishment of transportation policy and programmes. Under the BTC and THC, SBG had been in charge of its own destiny, returning satisfactory profits to its London masters with little outside interference. Even in the early STG days, the Scottish Office seemed more concerned about the group's socially-essential shipping services, and the bus companies were allowed to get on with it. The regulated regime meant that competition from other bus operators was absolutely minimal, and annual fares increases kept pace with the economy. Now Regional officials and politicians had been given a significant influence on what the group was doing and, in return for revenue support from the Regions, which had powers to reimburse the operational shortfall to bus companies, SBG had to work with the Regions and provide much information that had previously been regarded as commercially sensitive. Added to this, the four Scottish Corporation bus fleets were now controlled by the Regions. Thus Grampian (Aberdeen), Lothian (Edinburgh) and Tayside (Dundee) had not only transport co-ordinating powers but also their own bus fleets. Glasgow Corporation's buses had passed to Greater Glasgow PTE (now Strathclyde PTE) in 1973.

The group's express service network grew considerably in the 1970s. In addition to the long-established flagship services to London from Edinburgh and Glasgow, the Lancashire services and the seasonal 'bucket-and-spade' services to seaside resorts, there were new London services from Fife and Aberdeen, a service linking Glasgow with Uig (Skye), and an increasing number of cross-Border links, often jointly with NBC's new National Express arm, using the growing motorway network.

Moris Little retired as STG Deputy Chairman and Managing Director in 1975, to be replaced by Ian Irwin, formerly Group Secretary. Ian Irwin remained in this post to the break-up of the group, ably guiding it through some of its most difficult years.

The opening of Buchanan bus station in 1976 gave SBG a useful modern terminal at the north end of central Glasgow, replacing the long-established but cramped Buchanan Street and Dundas Street premises. Another bus station had been included in the redevelopment of the Anderston area, southwest of the city centre; while this replaced the Carlton Terrace and Clyde Street stances and Waterloo Street bus station, it was

never the most attractive site. Buchanan, on the other hand, survives and has undergone an expensive transformation by its new owners, Strathclyde PTE.

The 1970s were difficult years for all bus companies, as they battled with ever-dropping passenger numbers, the effects of inflation, militant trades unions and delays in vehicle deliveries. Over the period 1969-1980 SBG passenger journeys dropped nearly 40%, from 555.7 million to 336.7 million; vehicle miles dropped by 26% from 168.2 million to 124.4 million; staff numbers dropped by 40% from 17,843 to 10,598, largely as a result of the spread of driver-only operation; and the fleet dropped by 23% from 4,721 to 3,635. The position was steadily worsening, and, unchecked, could only deteriorate further.

One answer was SCOTMAP, the Scottish Market Analysis Project. Based on NBC's pioneering MAP surveys, SCOTMAP called on this experience and benefited from it. SBG decided to apply market analysis techniques to satisfy itself that bus services were in line with passenger demand, something that was becoming increasingly necessary if the group was seeking local or national government revenue support.

▲ After it had built up a fleet of 440 Leyland Leopards, Central moved on to new-generation single-deck chassis. Most were Gardner-engined Leyland Tigers, but there were also 10 Dennis Dorchesters, a Gardner underfloor-engined model that was developed largely for SBG. Five received dual-purpose Alexander TE bodies, but five, like DD5 (A105 RGE), received Alexander TS-type 53-seat bodies; the TS was a TE variant that was (perhaps understandably) favoured by Central over the P-type body that was sold to other group fleets at the time. *Alexander*

The Leyland National was bought new by all of the SBG fleets except Western, which eventually received second-hand examples. Alexander (Fife) Cowdenbeath (C) depot's FPN14 (RSG 814V), a 1980 NL116L11/1R 52-seater, carries an overall advertising livery for the Fife-London services, which also served Falkirk.
Gavin Booth collection

SCOTMAP involved on-bus passenger demand and bus journey time surveys, passenger attitude surveys, computer processing, analysis of passenger demand and revenue, replanning services and defining vehicle requirements, developing traffic management proposals, defining platform staff requirements and crew scheduling, developing fares and marketing policies, implementing the changes and monitoring them. This was a major exercise affecting all aspects of SBG's operations, and SCOTMAP planning began late in 1979 with the first surveys conducted in 1980. A new tier of senior management was introduced in each company, so that, in addition to the Traffic Manager, Chief Engineer and Company Secretary, there was now a Planning & Development Officer whose initial remit was to oversee the SCOTMAP functions.

The gradual growth of SBG's express services was further accelerated with their deregulation in 1980. In August 1983, Western Ayr (A) based AS2645 (RCS 699R), a 1977 Seddon Pennine VII with Alexander T-type 49-seat body, is seen leaving Cheltenham coach station for Glasgow, as part of the famous 3.00pm mass departure. An Eastern Scottish Seddon Pennine VII/ Plaxton Supreme IV can be seen in the background among National Express vehicles. *T. W. Moore*

30

This was a major market research exercise, and, while it confirmed that much of what SBG had been achieving by less scientific means was appropriate, there was also scope to redesign some service networks to take account of the travel patterns the surveys revealed. Although there are still those who are convinced that the SCOTMAP exercise was unnecessary, there are others who believe that it prepared SBG for the even tougher and less-controllable regime of the 1980s.

SBG responded to the 1980 Transport Act (which deregulated express services) with new coaches and cheaper fares, and the fresh interest in coaching that this generated led in 1983 to the creation of a marketing identity for the group's express services — Scottish Citylink. Instead of each SBG company running its own-liveried coaches on express duties, SBG went down the National Express route and faced up to the constant threat of competition with a new blue/yellow livery and a new coach specification.

Another product of express deregulation in Scotland was Stagecoach, which started by competing with SBG's Scotland-London services and went on to build up a massive empire, buying up three SBG companies in the process.

The Thatcher Government had made its attitude to deregulation and privatisation very clear, and in the bus industry there were two distinct camps — those who welcomed the opportunities and those who wanted to stick with the status quo. Against this uncertainty, SBG decided to restructure in 1985. The seven-company SBG of the past 24 years would become 11 bus companies and one coaching company.

Only the Fife company escaped any change, except to its name. In the late 1970s a corporate style of blue fleetname had been adopted with the company name followed by the word

'SCOTTISH'; now these names were adopted as company names, followed by 'Omnibuses Ltd'. So, for example, W. Alexander & Sons (Fife) Ltd became Fife Scottish Omnibuses Ltd.

The changes to the other companies were fairly major. Starting in the north, Highland's Oban area reverted to Midland; Northern lost its Tayside services to a new company, Strathtay; Midland lost its Perth area services to Strathtay and its services north of Glasgow to the new Kelvin company, while gaining Bo'ness and Linlithgow from Eastern, and Argyll and Islay from Western; Eastern lost its East Lothian and Borders operation to the new Lowland company, its Airdrie services to Central and had already lost its east Glasgow operations to Midland; Central lost its North Bank services to Kelvin; Western lost its northern part to the new Clydeside company. At the same time Scottish Citylink Coaches Ltd became a company in its own right.

The four new companies chose liveries that owed something to their 'parent' companies. Thus Clydeside went for a striking bright red/yellow; Kelvin initially went for a restrained light blue/azure blue but later opted for a more striking blue/yellow

The 1983 launch of the Scottish Citylink brand brought a common livery to SBG's express coaches. This is the prototype Alexander TC-type body, an improved version of the T-type, with fixed glazing and a one-piece door. It was shown at the 1983 Scottish Show with this non-standard fleetname style. A 47-seater based on Leyland Tiger TRBTL11/2RP chassis, it was delivered as Alexander (Midland) MPT120 (A120 GLS). *Alexander*

Leyland was keen to sell its new Olympian to SBG, where previously it had supplied Fleetlines. This is the pre-production Olympian/ECW that was registered OMS 910W and joined the Northern fleet as NLO1. It was first shown at the 1980 Motor Show in a version of Midland livery. This bus also appears in this book in Grampian Scottish livery. *Gavin Booth collection*

31

In 1979 Western Scottish was drafted in to the island of Islay, to provide services after the existing operator withdrew. Western shipped four Leyland Leopard PSU3E/4Rs with 55-seat Duple Dominant Express bodies to Islay (Y). These had been acquired with the business of Paton, Renfrew, that same year. YL8, 10, 9 (SSU 397R, YHS 282/1S) are seen with 'Islay Western SCOTTISH' fleetnames. *Gavin Booth collection*

There were still well over 300 prewar and wartime buses in the Alexanders fleet when it was split into three in 1961. Many were Leyland TS-type Tigers and Alexander (Northern) P533 (WG 8112), a 1939 Tiger TS8 with 35-seat Alexander body, is seen at Seagate bus station, Dundee, in June 1962 alongside 1950 Leyland Tiger PS1/Alexander PA161. By this time these buses were strictly NP533 and NPA161. Note the orange-backed Dundee depot code plate on both buses. NP533 would be withdrawn in 1963, but NPA161 survived until 1971. *Iain MacGregor*

scheme; Lowland went for green/yellow, initially with a paler green; Strathtay went for azure blue/marigold.

The 1985 changes would not be the last reorganisation of SBG. In 1989 Kelvin and Central were combined as Kelvin Central Buses Ltd, and Clydeside disappeared back into Western. However, the writing was on the wall for SBG. Its response to deregulation of bus services in 1986 was mixed. It put up a spirited fight in some areas, using minibuses and ex-London Routemasters in many places, while in others it lost out as other operators expanded. This was being played out against a background of great uncertainty, as SBG watched the NBC privatisation process taking place, with success for management buy-outs in many cases, but also the emergence of the new breed of super-group. SBG made out a strong case for privatisation as a single unit, but this would have gone

against the political dogma of the time. Plans were in place for an extensive reorganisation to produce a leaner, fitter group, but the inevitable happened in 1989 when the SBG privatisation was announced.

By 1991 all of the group companies had been sold, and, while initially management/employee buy-outs enjoyed some success, the realities of bus operation in the economic uncertainties of the early 1990s meant that they succumbed to approaches from other groups. Highland is now part of the Rapson's group; Northern, Fife and Western are Stagecoach companies; Strathtay has stayed with Traction Group; Eastern, Lowland and Midland went to Grampian (now FirstGroup); Kelvin Central is now part of First Glasgow, and Clydeside (which had been reformed after Western was privatised) is now 'Arriva Scotland West'.

Older Leylands could also be found in the new Alexander (Fife) company. FP669 (WG 9505), a 1940 Leyland TS8 Special with 39-seat Alexander body, is seen at Kirkcaldy's town service bus station in March 1963. The TS8 Special had a short driver's cab, increasing the saloon area and allowing 39 seats, four more than was possible on conventional vehicles. Alexanders received 106 TS8 Specials in 1939/40. FP669 was withdrawn later in 1963. Note the green-backed K (Kirkcaldy) depot plate. *Iain MacGregor*

Alexanders received over 100 utility Guy Arabs between 1942 and 1945, and later bought over 50 more from London Transport. This is one of its own 1944 examples, Alexander (Midland) RO530 (AMS 276), a Guy Arab II with Northern Counties 56-seat highbridge body, at Kinnoull Street, Perth in July 1962, painted in the 'town red' livery used for Perth's town service routes. This bus was withdrawn the following year. Like many of the older buses in the three Alexander fleets after the three-way split in 1961, RO530 was strictly MRO530 but did not carry its newly-prefixed number. It displays its blue-backed P (Perth) depot plate. *Iain MacGregor*

In 1949 Western SMT adopted a fleet numbering system with new deliveries starting at 601. One of the first buses delivered new with a number was DL602 (CSD 8), a 1949 Leyland Tiger PS1 with 35-seat Alexander body. The D in the fleetnumber indicates a Dumfries depot bus and the L stands for Leyland single-decker. Leyland double-deckers were coded D — where possible Western used the first letter of the chassis-maker's name for single-deckers and the last letter for double-deckers. DL602 is seen at Whitesands, for many years the bus terminal in Dumfries. *Harry Hay*

Transferred to the new Highland Omnibuses company in 1952 from Highland Transport, K57 (BST 917), a 1947 Guy Arab III with 34-seat rear-entrance Guy body, is seen in its last year in service at Farraline Park bus station, Inverness, in August 1962 beside new AEC Reliance/Alexander B38. Highland's fleet numbering system largely followed that of its parent company, Scottish Omnibuses. The DR depot code indicates a Dornoch-allocated bus. *Iain MacGregor*

36

Wearing the attractive light green/cream adopted by Scottish Omnibuses in 1949 is BB79 (GSF 662), an AEC Regent III 9612E with 53-seat Duple lowbridge bodywork. There were 20 of these Duple Regents and 20 Burlingham-bodied Regent IIIs bought in 1950, represented by BB94 on the right. They are seen at Edinburgh's St Andrew Square bus station in March 1964. The letter A after their fleetnumbers indicates that they are allocated to the company's main depot, New Street in Edinburgh. Both buses lasted with SOL until 1966/7. *Iain MacGregor*

37

Between 1947 and 1952 Central SMT bought 136 Leyland Titans of the 7.4-litre engine PD1 and PD1A varieties. At the same time it bought 110 of the bigger-engined PD2/1 model, though it reverted to PD1As after its first big PD2/1 delivery in 1948. L331 (CVD 531), a 1951 PD1A with Northern Counties 53-seat lowbridge body, is seen climbing Kilbowie Road, Clydebank, in April 1965, the year before it was withdrawn. Central's fleet numbering system was fairly simple — normally a single-letter type prefix and a numbering series for each that started at 1. No depot code was carried. *Iain MacGregor*

◄ In the stunning cream/yellow livery of Alexander (Northern), ND19 (BMS 414), a 1948 Daimler CVD6 with 33-seat Burlingham coach body, stands outside the company's Stonehaven (S) depot. These attractive vehicles had long lives — ND19 was withdrawn in 1970, and is one of three of these coaches that have been preserved. *Harry Hay*

39

▲ One of the first buses to be painted in the new Alexander (Northern) yellow/cream livery was NA77 (BMS 463), a 1948 AEC Regal I O662 with 35-seat Burlingham bus body. It is seen alongside similar A14, still in Alexanders blue, in Blairgowrie (BL) depot in June 1962. *Iain MacGregor*

Alexanders bought over 200 Leyland Tiger PS1s between 1947 and 1950, the majority with Alexander 35-seat bodies. Alexander (Fife) FPA35 (AWG 710) emerges from the 'country' bus station on Kirkcaldy Esplanade in March 1963. Delivered in 1947, it survived until 1968. *Iain MacGregor*

Over 100 buses from Young's of Paisley boosted the Western SMT fleet in 1951. All but one had distinctive XS registrations, and some could be found in the Western fleet until 1968. Based at the former Young's depot at Johnstone (J), JR2213 (XS 6756), a Daimler CVG6 with Northern Counties 56-seat highbridge body, was new to Young's in 1949, and is seen near Gilmour Street station, Paisley, in March 1962. This bus lasted with Western until 1964. *Iain MacGregor*

41

▲ Alexanders continued to buy front-engined Leyland single-deckers into the early part of the underfloor era. In 1952 it bought — doubtless at a bargain price — 20 Tiger OPS2/1 chassis that had been built in 1948, and these were given Alexander 35-seat coach bodies. In 1960, 17 of them lost their O.600 drivelines and received PS1 drivelines in their place; the OPS2/1 parts were used in the construction of 17 'new' double-deck PD3/3c Titans. MPB4 (DMS 817) is seen at Kirkintilloch (KH) depot after conversion, with a PS1 radiator and narrower axles. Beside it is a David Lawson-liveried Bristol Lodekka. *Iain MacGregor*

Four months after the 20 PBs were delivered to Alexanders, the company received the first of 84 Leyland Royal Tiger PSU1/15 coaches, most with Alexander 41-seat centre-entrance 'Coronation' bodies like NPC1 (BMS 222) of Alexander (Northern), seen leaving Aberdeen's Guild Street bus station. NPC1 was withdrawn in 1972 but is now preserved at the Scottish Vintage Bus Museum at Lathalmond, Fife. *Harry Hay*

Alexander 'Coronation'-style bodies were also built for Central SMT and Western SMT on Guy Arab chassis in 1952-4. Western MG967 (EAG 469), a 1952 Arab UF with centre-entrance 41-seat coach body, is seen in July 1963 outside the KLM airline office in Buchanan Street, Glasgow. This vehicle was one of 36 UFs that saw further service with Highland Omnibuses after they were withdrawn by Western in 1963-5. The M depot code prefix described Newton Mearns depot, replaced in 1968 by new premises at Thornliebank, still coded M. *Iain MacGregor*

43

Ever conscious of the need to economise, SBG enthusiastically moved on to the new lighter-weight single-deck underfloor-engined chassis that appeared in the early 1950s, particularly the AEC Reliance and Leyland Tiger Cub. Reliances were popular in the Alexanders Southern and Northern areas, and Aberdeen (A) based Alexander (Northern) NAC92 (HMS 241), a 1956 Reliance MU3RV with 45-seat Alexander bus body, is seen in Aberdeen. This style of Alexander bus body was built primarily for SBG companies. *Harry Hay*

Western SMT received over 50 utility Guy Arabs during the war years and continued to buy Guys until 1956, when it turned to Bristols for its Gardner-engined requirements. JY1172 (GSD 693), a 1955 Guy Arab IV with 55-seat Northern Counties lowbridge bodywork, is seen in Paisley on a local service. Northern Counties bodies continued to be a popular choice with Western until the late 1970s. *Harry Hay*

44

The Kirkintilloch-based bus operator David Lawson Ltd was taken over by Alexanders in 1936, but continued to operate as a separate Alexanders subsidiary until the 1961 reorganisation. Between 1956 and 1959, 27 Bristol LD6G Lodekkas with 60-seat Eastern Coach Works bodies were placed directly into the Lawson fleet, painted red/cream, but numbered in a common series with buses for the main Alexanders fleet. RD20 (GWG 996) is seen at Glasgow's Dundas Street bus station in April 1962, by which time it was strictly MRD20.
Iain MacGregor

Displaying one of the hallmarks of SBG buses over the years — paper destination stickers — Central SMT L494 (GM 7194) heads out through Yoker towards Old Kilpatrick, on the north bank of the Clyde, past posters for two staples of the Scottish diet, McEwan's beer and Mother's Pride bread. It is a 1955 Leyland Titan PD2/10 with 55-seat Northern Counties bodywork. This was one of Central's last exposed-radiator buses; the following year its Titans had Midland Red-style 'tin' fronts. *Iain MacGregor*

As a state-owned company, SBG could purchase all Bristol/ECW models, the Lodekka being by far the most popular. Although the flat-floor F-series models were the standard Lodekka models from 1960, SBG companies stuck to the previous LD-type until 1961. Western did receive a small batch of flat-floor types in 1961, including three FS6Gs like JB1627 (RAG 393) seen in the Clyde seaside resort of Largs on the local service in June 1963. Western only had three FS types; in 1962 it moved on to the longer FLF model. A small depot/bus station at Largs was treated as a sub-depot of Johnstone, hence the J prefix. *Iain MacGregor*

▲ The assortment of buses acquired by Scottish Omnibuses with the business of Lowland Motorways, Glasgow, in 1958 included two of these 1939 Leyland Titan TD5s with distinctive 1948 ECW 54-seat 'Beverley Bar' bodies, formerly with East Yorkshire. HH2H (GAT 61) is seen at Airdrie bus park in March 1962, the year it was withdrawn. The H prefix identified a Leyland in SOL's numbering scheme, HH being a double-decker. The H suffix was the code for Airdrie (Clarkston) depot. *Iain MacGregor*

48

One of the first new vehicles placed in service by Alexander (Midland) after the 1961 split was MPD213 (RMS 702), a Leyland Tiger Cub PSUC1/2 with a distinctive style of Alexander 38-seat coach body, new in July of that year. Only 20 bodies of this style were built. MPD213 is seen in September 1967 at Moffat, which is still a popular stopping-place for coach tours today. The SS depot code indicates Stepps depot, to the northeast of Glasgow. *Mark Page*

Coach touring was a particularly important part of the Alexanders and Scottish Omnibuses fleets, and in 1961/2 SOL bought 11 AEC Reliance 2MU3RV models with 34-seat Burlingham Seagull 70 coach bodies. They carried a distinctive maroon/cream livery and bore names of characters from the novels of Sir Walter Scott. B5 (WSF 205) — named *Lady of the Lake* — is seen when new leaving Edinburgh's St Andrew Square bus station on an afternoon tour to North Berwick and Dunbar, popular resorts on the East Lothian coast. *Gavin Booth collection*

Central SMT's most notable acquisition was the fleet of J. Laurie of Hamilton, trading as Chieftain. Sixteen ex-London Transport RTL-type Leyland PD2s passed into the Central fleet with the business in 1961. HL191 (JXN 333) is seen in the growing new town of East Kilbride in April 1962. It had been London RTL13 and lasted with Central until 1966. The HL fleetnumber signified that it was a highbridge vehicle, like most of the ex-Laurie buses, which were joining an otherwise lowbridge or lowheight double-deck fleet. *Iain MacGregor*

The first new buses for Alexander (Northern) were seven Leyland Titan PD3A/3s with 67-seat Alexander lowbridge bodies in 1961. Although they were similar to previous deliveries, the Aberdeen registrations symbolised the company's new independence. Elgin (E) based NRB281 (RRS 591) is seen at the Royal Naval Air Station at Lossiemouth in July 1970. *Iain MacGregor*

Alexander (Northern) mopped up a number of local bus operators in a series of takeovers in 1965-7, bringing some unusual vehicles into the fleet. Among the mixed inheritance from Simpson, Rosehearty in 1966 were eight of these Leyland Tiger PS1s with 59-seat Roe highbridge bodies. They had been new as single-deckers to Yorkshire Traction and County Motors of Lepton, rebuilt as double-deckers in 1955/6 and reregistered. NRA103 (HHE 320) is seen in Fraserburgh, still in Simpson green but with painted-on Northern fleetnumber 'plate'. This bus lasted with Northern until 1971. *Harry Hay*

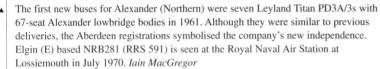

From 1955 Central SMT dual-sourced its main requirements from Bristol and Leyland. The Bristols were Lodekkas until 1967, then an ill-fated batch of VRTs in 1969. The Leylands were lowbridge Titans, then Albion Lowlanders, then Leopards.

At Biggar on the lengthy Glasgow-Peebles service is BE227 (CGM 727C), a 1965 Bristol FLF6G Lodekka with 68-seat ECW body. *Mark Page*

SBG's dissatisfaction with the rear-engined Bristol VRT double-deck chassis led the group to negotiate an exchange with FLF Lodekkas from National Bus Company fleets. A smartly-presented Central SMT BE370 (MNG 343E), a 1967 FLF6G with 70-seat ECW body, is seen passing the Ravenscraig steelworks near Motherwell in 1977. Once fitted with standard SBG-style destination indicators, these FLFs looked very much at home in Scotland. BE370 entered service with Central in 1973.
Mark Page

Central's move to 53-seat single-deckers in the 1970s was partly because it saw these as replacing 55-seat lowbridge double-deckers almost on a seat-for-seat basis, with the added 'benefit' of extra standing capacity. But it may have had something to do with the difficulty it appeared to have finding double-deck models that would suit its demanding requirements. Only the Lodekka, and later the Dominator, seemed to enjoy any real success, and in the meantime the company had tried — and quickly cascaded to other companies — Albion Lowlanders, Bristol VRTs and Daimler Fleetlines. This LR1 Lowlander, A22 (FGM 22) with Northern Counties 71-seat forward-entrance body, seen at Faifley in April 1965, was one of 30 Lowlanders bought in 1962/3 which by the end of 1965 had been farmed out to SBG's Fife and Highland companies.
Iain MacGregor

Dissatisfaction with Leyland's double-deck offerings led SBG to work with Volvo importer Ailsa Trucks, to develop a new front-engined double-decker for the group's use. Although SBG envisaged something more like the Bristol FLF reborn, Ailsa Trucks had its eye on a wider market, and the Ailsa was launched. It had its engine at the front, but was only practical in full-height form — restricting its appeal for SBG, which had routes and depots with height restrictions. In spite of this, SBG companies received substantial Ailsa deliveries and found suitable routes and depots for them. The first major deliveries were to Alexander (Fife), which received 40 in 1975, all with 79-seat Alexander bodies. FRA21 (LSX 21P) is seen in Dunfermline in October 1975. The Ailsa gave many years of hard-working service to SBG fleets. *Gavin Booth*

The Daimler Fleetline was SBG's standard lowheight double-deck model; these were bodied by Alexander, Northern Counties and ECW. In 1971 Central received 35 CRG6LXB models with ECW 77-seat bodies, such as D8 (TGM 208J), seen in Glasgow in 1973; like other Central double-deckers these were cascaded to other SBG fleets, which were happy to receive them. *Mark Page*

54

Midland received just 14 Ailsas, which worked in the Perth area. MRA6 (YMS 706R) is seen in Perth in 1977, when new. It has Alexander AV-type 79-seat bodywork.
Mark Page

Highland adopted this striking peacock blue/poppy red livery in 1970. Although the company continued to receive cast-offs from other SBG companies, it received a growing number of new vehicles, mostly Bedfords and Fords for several years before moving on to heavyweights. Seen at Uig Pier on Skye in 1977, after completing the long journey from Glasgow, T104 (HST 204N) was a 1975 Ford R1114 with the ubiquitous Alexander Y-type body, in this case fitted out as a 49-seat coach. The P depot plate signifies Portree depot, on Skye. At Uig the coach linked with Caledonian MacBrayne ferries to Harris and North Uist. *Mark Page*

56

In 1976 SBG decided to adopt a common livery for its growing group of Scotland-London express services, inspired no doubt by the spread of the National Express brand in England and Wales. A blue/white livery was applied to the London coaches of the Eastern, Fife, Northern and Western companies, complete with a new 'SCOTTISH' fleetname featuring a three-quarter saltire. The first journey by a blue/white-liveried coach was on 31 March 1976, when Scottish Omnibuses XA364A (SFS 364H) was unveiled at St Andrew Square bus station, Edinburgh, before setting out on the daytime service to London. It is a 1970 Bristol REMH6G with Alexander M-type 42-seat bodywork, a distinctive body design developed for the group, featuring high-set double-glazed windows, features that were ahead of their time. This coach had been painted in a striking yellow/black livery when new. The M-type was also built for SBG companies on Leyland Leopard, Seddon Pennine VII and Volvo B58 chassis. The X prefix to the Bristol (A) type code indicated that it was a London service vehicle; a Y prefix indicated a coach, and Z a dual-purpose vehicle. No prefix signified a service bus. *Gavin Booth*

57

After resisting the charms of the Leyland National for a number of years, SBG finally succumbed in 1977 when Eastern received a batch to help overcome a vehicle shortage. Kirkcaldy-based Fife FPN6 (HSC 106T), a 1978 11351A/1R 49-seater, is seen when new in October 1978 at Kirkcaldy bus station, with a typical SBG destination sticker in the front windscreen. It carries Fife Scottish fleetnames in the corporate style adopted in 1978. *Gavin Booth*

To publicise its 1979 new vehicle orders, SBG organised a line-up of current and planned vehicle types at Buchanan bus station in May 1978. These included recent deliveries to group companies, and demonstrators provided by manufacturers eager to impress the group. From the right are: Fife Leyland Leopard/Duple Dominant; Highland Ford R1114/Duple Dominant; Western Volvo B58/Alexander M-type; Western Fleetline/Northern Counties; Leyland Titan/Park Royal demonstrator; West Midlands PTE MCW Metrobus; Central Leopard/Alexander Y-type; Eastern Seddon Pennine VII/Plaxton Supreme; Eastern Leyland National; Northern Leopard/Duple Dominant; Midland Volvo Ailsa/Alexander. The group did buy Metrobuses, and while it had Titans on order for the Fife company, these were never built, and the group settled on Olympians instead. *Gavin Booth*

In the 1970s SBG companies mounted a series of open days to promote the group's role, particularly following Scotland's regionalisation in 1975. At one of these events, at Fife's central workshops at Esplanade, Kirkcaldy in October 1978, a number of company buses sit over the pits. From the right these are a Bristol Lodekka/ECW, an Albion Viking/Alexander Y-type, a Daimler Fleetline/Alexander, a Volvo Ailsa/Alexander, an AEC breakdown wagon and an AEC Reliance/Alexander Y-type. *Gavin Booth*

Another SBG open day coincided with the opening of a new bus station/depot in the West Lothian new town of Livingston in May 1979. Over the pristine pits at Livingston are, from the left, a Seddon Pennine VII/Alexander Y-type, a Daimler Fleetline/ECW, FLF- and FS-type Bristol Lodekkas and another Fleetline. Scottish Omnibuses had adopted the fleetname 'Eastern Scottish' in 1964. *Gavin Booth*

To determine its future double-deck policy, SBG conducted a series of trials with four different models in 1980. Three new-generation types — Dennis Dominator, MCW Metrobus and Volvo Ailsa — were compared with the established Leyland Fleetline model, working on Glasgow-area services out of Midland's Milngavie depot. Lined up ready to do battle in a January 1980 snowstorm are the buses, prominently labelled TB1-4. TB1 is a normal Midland Fleetline/ECW; TB2 is Midland's first Metrobus/Alexander; TB3 is actually a Fife Ailsa/Alexander painted as a Midland

vehicle; and TB4 is Central's prototype Dominator/Alexander, wearing an advertising livery. In fuel consumption terms, the Fleetline came out best (7.26mpg), followed by the Metrobus (6.2mpg), Dominator (6.03mpg) and Ailsa (5.8mpg). The arrival of the Leyland Olympian prompted a second series of tests. Again the Fleetline came out on top (7.36mpg), followed by the Olympian (6.51mpg), Metrobus (6.14mpg) and Ailsa (5.82mpg). *Gavin Booth*

The body production lines at Alexander's Glasgow Road, Falkirk, coachworks were kept busy with orders from SBG companies and a number of other important customers. This May 1976 view shows SBG T-type bodies (nearest and third lines) and D-type bodies on Daimler Fleetline (farthest line). In between are AL bodies on Leyland Atlantean for Greater Glasgow and Lothian. *Gavin Booth*

At Dunbeg, en route to Oban, Midland MPE150 (CMS 380L), a Stepps-allocated 1972 Leyland Leopard PSU3/3R with Alexander Y-type 49-seat coach body. The Y-type Leopard was SBG's workhorse for many years, with thousands operating around Scotland. This bus carries the corporate 'Midland SCOTTISH' fleetname on the nearside, as well as the traditional Alexanders bluebird logo, and an older-style 'Midland' name on the front.
Mark Page

The Seddon Pennine VII chassis was developed for SBG as a Gardner-engined alternative to the Leopard, which Leyland was reluctant to supply with the engineer's favourite 6HLXB engine. Western RS2648 (RCS 703R) is a 1977 Pennine with the recently-introduced Alexander T-type dual-purpose body, and is seen at Rothesay Pier in May 1982 awaiting day-trippers on the ferry from Wemyss Bay for the Round Bute Tour. The vehicle carries a Western variation on the corporate fleetname — black lettering but blue saltire — and the revised black/white livery that included shades of grey. The R prefix indicated the Pointhouse depot at Rothesay, originally built for horse trams in 1882.
Gavin Booth

64

Western's mainland operations often required high-capacity buses, although none had as many seats as seven 33ft-long Daimler Fleetlines bought in 1967. Six, like JR2101 (GCS 162E) seen here on a Paisley local service, had 83-seat Northern Counties bodies. *Mark Page*

Central tended to need high-capacity buses, but had a limited requirement for smaller buses in the East Kilbride area, which by this time had become the company's most profitable operation. In East Kilbride in September 1981 is FS2 (RUS 815W) a Ford A0609 with Alexander (Belfast) S-type 27-seat body, representing an early midibus type that did not prove entirely successful. *Gavin Booth*

Highland progressed to new heavyweight buses from the late 1970s, first with Leyland Fleetlines and then with Leyland National 2s like N18 (AST 160W), a 1981 Oban (O) based 49-seater seen here in 1982 on an Oban local service. Highland dropped the peacock blue colour at this time, simplifying its livery to poppy red/grey. *Mark Page*

66

Northern was used for experiments to find a new lighter-weight chassis to succeed the Fords and, to a lesser degree, Bedfords that SBG used on less-demanding work. In 1982/3 Volvo supplied a B57 and Dennis a Lancet, and these were fitted with the last two Alexander Y-type bodies to be built. A further five Lancets were ordered for 1984. ND4 (A504 FSS) was one of these, a Lancet SDA516 model with high-built Alexander P-type 53-seat bodywork, seen in Montrose (M) in 1984. The rather basic P-type body was introduced as successor to the hugely-successful Y-type, and only came into its own when it was developed into the PS-type, which became the standard single-deck model for the Stagecoach and Mainline groups for a number of years. The privatisation of SBG meant that no further middleweight buses were required.
Mark Page

68

Grampian Scottish was a short-lived co-ordination between Alexander (Northern) and Grampian Regional Transport, whereby the vehicles used on Aberdeen local services by both operators wore Grampian's green/cream livery, but carried SBG-style fleetnames. Introduced in 1983, it was discontinued in 1986. Wearing the livery, but with a 'broadside' advert, is Northern NLO1 (OMS 910W), a most significant bus. New in 1980, it was one of the prototype Leyland Olympians (chassis B45.04) and carried ECW 77-seat lowheight bodywork. It was initially loaned to SBG, painted in Midland colours, and demonstrated with group companies, but eventually joined Alexander (Northern), which went on to build up a substantial Olympian fleet. Seen in 1984, it later passed to the Clydeside company.
Mark Page

69

Coach touring still figured in SBG's plans, but changing travel and leisure patterns meant that passenger numbers were falling. At South Queensferry, in the shadow of the Forth Bridge, in September 1981 is Galashiels-based Eastern Scottish ZS961D (OSF 961V), a new Seddon Pennine VII with Plaxton Supreme IV Express bodywork. Although SBG had traditionally bought Duple coach bodies, it turned to Plaxton in 1977 to help overcome a body shortage, and Plaxton went on to become a significant supplier. History dictated that Galashiels vehicles carried the D depot code, while the more obvious G was allocated to Dalkeith. *Gavin Booth*

A more mundane Eastern Scottish vehicle, Seddon Pennine VII/Alexander Y-type S634N (YSG 634W), new in 1980 and seen in Motherwell in 1981 on the long 27 route to Edinburgh. Although Eastern bought Leyland Leopards between 1969 and 1975, it preferred the Gardner-engined Seddon for its single-deck bus and coach work until 1982. The code N indicated the new Livingston depot built in 1979. *Mark Page*

Express coach service deregulation in 1980 brought competition to the Scotland-London routes and prompted SBG to fight back with new coaches and lower fares. The first new coaches were to a body style developed by Duple for SBG, the Dominant III; this was a development of its existing Dominant II but with small, double-glazed windows in the style of SBG's Alexander M-types. The first Dominant III for SBG was also one of the first examples of Leyland's new Tiger, the more powerful, air-suspension chassis built to compete with Volvo's B10M. This coach, Eastern Scottish XH544A (BSG 544W) was one of three prototype Tigers shipped out to Morocco in 1981 for the lavish Tiger launch. It is seen at Edinburgh's St Andrew Square bus station in April 1982 preparing to leave on its overnight journey to London. *Gavin Booth*

71

Express deregulation brought double-deck coaches on to Scotland-London services, notably those of the infant Stagecoach company. SBG turned to MCW for a competitor, and the Metroliner was born. The first was TSX 1Y, built in 1982, which was initially demonstrated to SBG and which later joined the Northern fleet. It is seen being piped out of Glasgow's Buchanan bus station on 6 April 1983 on its inaugural trip to London. These 69-seat coaches were impressive, but ultimately proved unreliable. The livery predated the blue/yellow adopted for Scottish Citylink later in 1983. *Gavin Booth*

Scottish Citylink was set up by SBG to market the group's express and longer-distance services under a common banner. A variety of coach types wore the blue/yellow livery, including Alexander TE-types like this 1983 Eastern Scottish Leyland Tiger TRBTL11/2RP 49-seater, CL329 (A329 BSC), seen turning on to Princes Street, Edinburgh on the popular 500 service linking Edinburgh with Glasgow, as well as Glasgow Airport and the Clyde coast at Gourock. Eastern adopted the C prefix to indicate Citylink vehicles. *Gavin Booth*

72

Minibuses started to infiltrate SBG from 1986, the time of local bus deregulation, and while most were Dodge/Renault S56s, Midland took four MCW Metrorider MF150/1s with 25-seat bodies. MM649 (D649 GLS) is seen when new in 1987. *Gavin Booth*

73

In preparation for deregulation, SBG reorganised its company structure in June 1985, creating four new companies from parts of others. Vehicles of two of the new companies, Kelvin and Lowland, are seen in Glasgow in June 1985 at the launch of the new liveries and the Best Bus campaign that coincided with this. Kelvin Scottish, operating to the north of Glasgow, initially adopted this restrained blue livery, and Lowland Scottish, operating in the eastern Borders, initially went for light green/yellow. The Kelvin bus is a 1982 MCW Metrobus with Alexander RL-type lowheight 78-seat body from the Midland fleet, and shows its first Kelvin number, M29 (ULS 629X). The Lowland bus is 314 (PSF 314Y), a 1982 Leyland Tiger TRBTL11/2R with 49-seat Alexander T-type body, formerly an Eastern Scottish bus. *Gavin Booth*

Lowland Scottish was the smallest of the new companies, and located its head office at Galashiels, next to the company's main depot. Outside the depot in August 1985 is 172 (BSF 772S), a 1977 Leyland National 52-seater. It wears the short-lived light green paint that was replaced by a more practical darker green. Lowland took over the Border and East Lothian area services of Eastern Scottish, and sensibly adopted G as the Galashiels depot code. *Gavin Booth*

Strathtay Scottish adopted a striking livery that combined the Midland blue with a strong tangerine shade, later relieved with white. At Perth bus station in June 1986 is SO2 (SSA 9X), a 1981 Leyland Olympian ONLXB/1R with Alexander RL-type 77-seat body, formerly in the Northern fleet. Strathtay inherited territory from the Northern and Midland companies. *Gavin Booth*

Kelvin Scottish was based on Glasgow-area services previously operated by Central and Midland. It soon ditched the original restrained livery in favour of a bolder scheme with a yellow front, seen here on an MCW Metrobus/Alexander RL, 1620 (ULS 620X), leaving Anderston bus station, Glasgow, in June 1987 alongside Central R18 (D818 RYS), a Dodge S56 with Alexander AM-type 25-seat body. Behind is a Kelvin Leyland National in the original livery, but with later yellow front. *Gavin Booth*

The Kelvin livery was later simplified as shown on 1943 (LDS 317A), a former London AEC Routemaster (RM367) photographed in Argyle Street, Glasgow, after Kelvin and Central had been merged as Kelvin Central Buses. *Gavin Booth*

Former London Routemasters were bought by Clydeside, Kelvin and Strathtay, but the Clydeside ones were the first and probably the best known. RM874 (WLT 874) still retained both its London fleet and registration numbers when seen in September 1986 in Glasgow's Union Street, crossing Argyle Street on the Paisley Road group of routes that were their home for a number of years. Clydeside's red/yellow livery suited the Routemasters well. *Gavin Booth*

78

Buchanan bus station was the busiest in Scotland, and a wide range of SBG buses could always be found there. This July 1987 view shows, in the foreground, Leopard/Y-types of Midland, Central and Kelvin, with a Northern MCW Metroliner coach returning to Aberdeen. In the bus station can be seen (on the left) Clydeside Routemasters and Leopards, and, with a black roof, a Clydeside Ailsa liveried for route 12; a Clydeside Fleetline receives attention on the right, sitting alongside a Kelvin Leopard/Dominant; in the background is a Central Tiger/Alexander TS, and the coaches in the top corner are a West Coast Motors Duple Caribbean and a Stagecoach Duple 320. The Fife double-decker in the centre is one of two Volvo Citybuses with Alexander RDC coach bodies. *Gavin Booth*

79

▲ Symbolising the end of SBG — two consecutively-numbered ex-Alexander (Northern) Leyland Olympian ONLXB/1Rs with Alexander RL 77-seat bodies sit at Stonehaven depot in 1991 after the company had been taken over by Stagecoach. LO4 (SSA 4X) wears Stagecoach stripes, while LO3 (SSA 3X) still wears its Northern yellow/cream. *Gavin Booth*

5. The SBG Fleet

The SMT Group had a mixed fleet of roundly 4,000 buses at the time of nationalisation. It had built up a reputation for shrewd vehicle purchasing and, although its prewar standardisation had been upset by the restrictions of World War 2 and the lack of real choice in the early postwar period, it was moving back to standardised types by 1949.

In 1949 the oldest buses in the fleets of the four group companies dated from the early 1930s, and there were numerous other prewar buses, some of which would complete a further 15 years' service before they were withdrawn. Although SBG purchases tend to suggest that the group was not at the cutting edge of new technology, the SMT group had switched enthusiastically to diesel engines in the 1930s while many other companies were still considering the advantages over petrol engines, and Alexanders had operated three twin-steer Leyland prototypes, two front-engined Gnus and a horizontal-engined Panda, but had sold these on by 1945/6. Although SBG adopted a rather more conservative vehicle policy than its opposite number in England and Wales (NBC), famously rejecting Bristol VRTs in favour of FLF Lodekkas, and turning to the Leyland National only when accumulated vehicle delivery delays and shortages forced it to do so, it did play its part in developing what became the Volvo Ailsa and Seddon Pennine VII, as well as adopting power-assisted steering and fully-automatic gearboxes in the 1970s.

Group vehicle orders were placed annually, and a glance back at these reveals that there was some centrally-imposed standardisation, but companies tried to plough their own individual furrows. SBG was a major target customer for the main manufacturers, and Leyland in particular courted the group with substantial discounts for large orders. Leyland even produced models that seemed to be aimed at SBG — like the Nimbus, Aberdonian, Lowlander and Viking — with varying degrees of success. Leyland's near-monopoly in the 1970s led to disquiet among many operators, and out of this was born the Ailsa and Pennine VII, both designed with co-operation from SBG. Other manufacturers managed to break into SBG orders. Bristol regularly supplied a proportion of the group's new vehicles from the mid-1950s, MCW supplied buses and coaches from the late 1970s, and Dennis was starting to make

an impact just as the group was winding up.

Alexander Coachbuilders had a head-start for the group's bodywork orders, but ECW, for obvious reasons, and Burlingham, Duple, Northern Counties, Park Royal and Plaxton did well at various times.

Scottish Omnibuses

A look round the 1949 group fleets reveals large numbers of Leylands, AECs and Guys, both single-deck and double-deck. Leylands figured in all four group fleets, but Scottish Omnibuses boasted a mixed fleet with a large proportion of AECs, the oldest dating back to 1932 when a substantial batch of Regals had been bought; most of these were still in service, mostly rebuilt or rebodied, and some survived until 1959. SMT had dual-sourced its single-deck requirements and also bought Leyland Tigers, and for most of its coach touring duties bought Bedfords. In 1938/9 it had bought all-Leyland Titan TD5 double-deckers, and these were its main 'modern' double-deckers until AEC Regals and Leyland Tigers received new Alexander double-deck bodies during the war. A few assorted 'unfrozen' buses had been delivered in the early years of the war, and some of these survived, and 60 Bedford OWBs and 22 Guy Arabs represented the utility intake. The Bedfords had all gone by 1950, but some of the Guys survived until 1958 — some even returned from Highland Omnibuses to work in Edinburgh in 1963 after some SOL Lodekkas were transferred to Highland.

SOL abandoned Leylands completely in the early postwar period; none was bought new between 1942 and 1957. Other than Bedford OB coaches, only AECs were bought between 1946 and 1953, apart from one very short-lived Austin in 1952. There were Regal and Regal III buses and coaches, and 80 Regent III lowbridge double-deckers, and in 1951, partly to counteract competition on the London services from Northern Roadways, SOL bought 26 Regal IV 30-seat coaches for the London service, the first underfloor-engined types in the group. Alexander, Burlingham and Duple were favoured for single-deck and double-deck bodies, and much rebodying and body-swapping took place in the early postwar period.

SOL's workshops could turn their hand to virtually anything

All of the SMT group fleets turned to rebuilding and rebodying late prewar vehicles to help them through the postwar vehicle shortage. In some cases, postwar buses were given new bodies, thus releasing bodies suitable for older chassis. Scottish Omnibuses H209W (SY 6024), a Leyland Tiger TS7, had been ordered by the Musselburgh & District (Coast Line) company, but was delivered new to SMT after the company was taken over in 1937. It received this 1949 Alexander body in 1954; the body had previously been mounted on an AEC Regal III, which then received a new full-fronted body. It is seen turning into St Andrew Square, Edinburgh, from the bus station in the late 1950s, and was withdrawn in 1960. The W depot code referred to Musselburgh. *Photobus*

and in 1952-4 constructed 23 'new' 30ft-long single-deckers from former London Transport utility Guy Arabs, five for its own fleet and 18 for Highland Omnibuses. It also built a small bus using Albion Claymore parts, which appeared in 1955, just at the time Albion was developing its similar Nimbus model.

AEC's domination of SOL's orders was to be challenged, however. Under state control the Scottish group could buy Bristol and ECW products, and Bristol LS6G coaches were chosen for coach duties in 1954/6, followed by MW6G coaches in 1958. These were to be SOL's only Bristol single-deckers until 1966, but the Bristol/ECW Lodekka became the company's standard double-decker from 1956 until 1966, with LD, FS and FLF models joining the fleet in significant numbers. The only non-standard double-deckers bought during this period were, ironically, Leyland Titan PD2/20s bought at short notice to provide tram replacement services beyond the Glasgow city boundary.

For single-deck bus and dual-purpose types in the 1950s SOL continued to favour AEC, first Monocoaches (SOL built up the largest fleet of this integral model) and then Reliances, with Park Royal and, increasingly, Alexander bodies. Burlingham bodies were chosen for a small batch of luxury touring coaches.

One of the first 36ft AEC Reliances, carrying one of the first Alexander Y-type bodies, was built for SOL's London services, to be followed in 1963/4 by more short and long Reliance/Y-types for a variety of duties.

The acquisition of Lowland Motorways in 1958 brought some unusual types into the SOL fleet; although most were painted into SOL green, some lasted only for a short time. Oddities included Daimler CWA6s, 'Beverley Bar'-roof Leyland TD5s and Cravens RTs. The RTs and some newer Leyland double-deckers lasted in the fleet for a few years, but two Leyland Tiger Cubs were quickly transferred to

82

Alexanders, where they were more at home.

When Baxter's was taken over in 1962 it had a considerably more up-to-date fleet, and there were new buses on order. The Baxter's fleet was a good fit for SOL, mainly consisting of AEC single-deckers and lowbridge Leyland double-deckers. One oddity that stayed in the SOL fleet was a 1961 AEC/Park Royal Bridgemaster, and Baxter's had two more Bridgemasters on order at the time of takeover. One appeared in 1963, but the other was diverted to Red Rover, Aylesbury, and a Renown was substituted. Also on order was a Daimler Fleetline, which joined the SOL fleet in 1963, the first new rear-engined vehicle in the Scottish group. After a short period of repainting Baxter's vehicles in SOL green, the local services in Airdrie and Coatbridge reverted to Baxter's blue and this arrangement survived for many years, with buses transferred from the main SOL fleet and painted into Baxter's blue.

Something similar happened when Stark's of Dunbar was taken over in 1964. There had always been a close relationship between SMT/SOL and Stark's. For years Stark's buses on the Dunbar-Edinburgh service were painted green and carried SMT fleetnames; Stark's local services in East Lothian used green-painted buses with Stark's fleetnames. Following the takeover, the Dunbar-Edinburgh buses were painted in light green and carried Stark's names. The Stark's fleet had received new Alexander-bodied buses for a number of years, but as it favoured Leylands these were often added on to Alexanders orders, and were largely to that company's specification rather than SMT's or SOL's as might seem more logical. Four Ford coaches were immediately transferred to the Highland fleet, and would be the first of many in this fleet, but the Stark's Leyland Tiger Cubs continued to work for the company where on previous form they might have been expected to reappear in one of the Alexanders fleets.

More than any other SBG company, SOL suffered regular vehicle shortages, and these were tackled by drafting in buses from other group companies, usually on a short-term basis. Most operated in their existing colours, but some lasted long enough to receive SOL green.

Bristol single-deckers reappeared in the SOL orders in 1966, with RELH6G coaches which carried Alexander Y-type bodies. These were followed in 1969/70 by 12m-long REMH6G coaches with striking Alexander M-type bodies for the

83

Decidedly unusual SOL deliveries in 1957 were 20 Leyland Titan PD2/20s with Park Royal lowbridge 56-seat bodies. The Edinburgh company had not bought a new Leyland since 1942, but needed buses quickly after Glasgow Corporation withdrew some tram services beyond the city boundary in November 1956. The 20 Leylands, on chassis intended for Edinburgh Corporation, were delivered in the early part of 1957 and were allocated to Airdrie (H) depot. HH548H (OWS 548) is seen when new in St Andrew Square, Edinburgh, before setting out on the long 310 route to Glasgow via Bathgate. Before Edinburgh bus station was built, the centre of the square was used as the city's main terminal point.
Gavin Booth collection

84

Edinburgh-London services. Other, less satisfactory Bristols were the VRTs bought in 1968/9. These included the first production VRTs — the only VRTLLs with ECW bodies. The VRTs proved unsatisfactory in Scotland and were exchanged with NBC Lodekka FLF6Gs in 1973.

SBG was looking at lighter-weight single-deckers at this time to replace the last of the front-engined AEC Regals and Leyland Tigers on less demanding duties. SOL opted for Bedfords, and between 1967 and 1975 bought VAM5, VAM70, YRQ and YRT models, many of which were used on services in the Borders. SOL also bought Bristol LH6Ps with Alexander bodies in 1970.

After its experience with the Bristol VRT, SOL turned to Daimler Fleetlines with ECW bodies, which became the standard double-decker in the 1970s. Similarly, after problems with the 1966 batch of AEC Reliances, SOL briefly turned to Leyland Leopards for its full-size single-deckers, before embracing a new model, designed for SBG as an antidote to Leyland's refusal to produce a Gardner-engined Leopard. This was the Seddon Pennine VII; SOL took the prototype in 1973

and went on to build up a substantial fleet of this type, including six with Alexander M-type bodies for London service. Most Seddons had Alexander Y-type or T-type bodies, but delivery delays forced the company to turn to Plaxton, which would supply coach bodies to the company for many years.

Deliveries to SOL got rather out of step in the 1970s, due to order backlogs at manufacturers and an erratic ordering pattern. Public disquiet over cancelled journeys due to non-availability of buses reached a head in 1978, and that year no fewer than 149 new buses entered service, including over 100 Seddons and some Volvo Ailsas. This new double-deck model had been designed by Ailsa Trucks at SBG's bidding, and featured a compact, front-mounted engine. SOL was an enthusiastic Ailsa fan, buying further batches until 1984; it also bought two batches of underfloor-engined Volvo Citybuses, as well as two batches of Leyland's Citybus competitor, the DAB-built Lion. All the Volvos and the Lions had Alexander bodies. SOL also bought Leyland Olympians from 1982, first with ECW bodies and then with Alexander — including two with coach bodies.

Another new Leyland model bought from 1981 was the underfloor-engined Tiger single-decker, chosen for coach duties with Duple and Plaxton bodies, and for bus work with Alexander TE-type bodies. SOL also bought the MCW Metroliner double-deck coach, a type initially developed for SBG, as well as the single-deck version of the Metroliner.

Alexanders

The oldest buses in the Alexanders fleet in 1949 dated nominally from 1929; these were rebuilt and rebodied Leyland Lions. Apart from Bedford coaches, Alexanders had bought Leylands almost exclusively, right through the 1930s — single-deck Cheetahs, Lions and Tigers and double-deck Titans — and vast numbers of these were still in the fleet in 1949, many ostensibly unrebuilt; some prewar Leylands would survive the 1961 split and continue in service until 1964.

During the war, apart from a few 'unfrozen' Leylands, Alexanders received Bedford OWBs and Guy Arabs, and a few Daimler CWA6s. Like all SMT group fleets it had prewar single-deckers rebodied with Alexander utility double-deck lowbridge bodies to give much-needed extra seating capacity. Before 1942 Alexander had not built double-deck bodies.

Immediately after the war, Alexanders took AEC Regal and Guy Arab single-deckers, followed by the first of over 200

◄ More than any other bus company in Scotland, SBG fleets could pull large numbers of vehicles out of the hat for special occasions. In George Square, Edinburgh, in 1972 a line of Eastern Scottish coaches collects delegates to a radiology conference for tours of the Scottish countryside. The leading coach, drafted in from Baillieston depot (C), is YH424C (YSC 424K), a 1972 Leyland Leopard PSU3/3R with Alexander Y-type 45-seat coach-seated body. After unfortunate experience with 590-engined AEC Reliances bought in 1966, in 1969-75 Eastern briefly favoured Leopards for its full-size single-deckers, before switching to the new Seddon Pennine VII.
Gavin Booth

85

An Alexanders contrast — Midland's new 1961 Stirling (S) allocated Leyland Tiger Cub PSUC1/2 PD207 (RMS 697), with 38-seat Alexander coach body, poses with Alexanders' former F55 (WG 1448), the 1932 Albion PW65 with Alexander bus body that was the subject of the first successful private bus preservation effort in Scotland. Nearly 30 years separates the buses, which are seen at Stirling on an Omnibus Society Scottish Branch tour. *Gavin Booth*

Leyland Tiger PS1s. There were Bedford OB, Commer Commando and Daimler CVD6 coaches; the first real postwar double-deckers were Leyland Titan PD1s, and there were 25 Guy Arab III double-deckers in 1948. Double-deck orders switched to the Leyland PD2 from 1950, though there were 20 AEC Regent III, in 1951.

The first production underfloor-engined vehicles — the solitary Leyland Panda had been sold by 1946 — were Leyland Royal Tiger coaches bought in 1952/3, but from 1954 Alexanders opted for the lighter Leyland Tiger Cub as well as the AEC Monocoach and Reliance, and smaller batches of Bristol LS6Gs and Guy Arab LUFs. Bristol Lodekkas first appeared in the fleet in 1956, and from 1958 Leyland Titans were the 30ft-long PD3 model.

After 1949 Alexanders acquired many vehicles on the secondhand market or from operators taken over. The logical transfer of SOL's Dundee area in 1949 brought 55 assorted Leyland single-deckers that fitted well into the main fleet. The takeover of Sutherland, Peterhead, in 1950 brought over 80 vehicles — AECs, Albions, Daimlers, Guys and Leylands — including some recent purchases that survived beyond the 1961 Alexander split. Thirty-seven ex-London Transport utility Guy Arabs were bought in 1952 and many of these operated, still with their original bodies, for a number of years; most were

used in dark red livery on Kirkcaldy and Perth town services.

The associated David Lawson company, which also used the dark red livery, had received what were essentially standard Alexanders vehicles, as well as transfers from the main fleet, from the late 1930s until 1960. In 1961 the Lawson business was merged into the new Alexander (Midland) company.

Like other Scottish group companies, Alexanders had extensive workshop facilities that allowed it to tackle virtually any major mechanical or bodybuilding task. In 1961 Alexanders used units from some of its Leyland Tiger PS1 and OPS2 single-deckers to construct new 30ft-long chassis on which were mounted new Alexander lowbridge double-deck bodies.

The sheer size of the Alexanders company and its fleet — around 1,800 at the time, and vying with Midland Red to be the biggest bus fleet in Britain outside London — led to the three-way split of the company in 1961. Although Alexanders had multi-sourced its requirements in the postwar years, it had a policy of keeping certain types in distinct areas, so when the new companies were formed they largely inherited the fleets operated in the old Southern, Fife and Northern Areas.

Leylands, Albions and Bedfords were to be found in all three Areas, but AECs and Daimlers were concentrated in Southern and Northern, Bristols and Guys (indeed all Gardner-

86

engined buses) in Southern and Fife, and Commers in Southern.

Alexander (Midland) had over 900 buses in 1961, making it the largest of the three Alexander companies. Its oldest buses dated from 1935 and, while these didn't last long, some prewar-type buses lasted until 1964, and utilities to 1965. Midland's first new vehicles, in 1961, were Leyland Tiger Cubs and Titans, and Bristol Lodekkas, continuing the previous buying pattern. A new type to appear was the Lowlander, yet another Albion chassis designed with SBG sales in mind. It was a lowheight bus in the Lodekka mould, and only featured in Midland orders in 1963. From 1964 the Leyland Leopard/Alexander Y-type became the standard single-decker, and the Midland Leopard fleet grew to over 400 buses.

The rear-engined Albion Viking VK43L was another attempt to provide a lighter-weight single-decker, and Midland bought 75 between 1965 and 1969 before switching to the Bristol LH6P in 1970 and the Ford R1014/R1114 from 1974.

After the Albion Lowlander, Midland turned to the Bristol Lodekka FLF6G, from 1963, and the Daimler Fleetline, from 1967. In 1970 it received 15 Bristol VRTs, but by the following year had swapped them with Eastern National for FLFs, the first SBG/NBC exchange of this type. Fourteen Volvo Ailsas were bought in 1977, but Midland then turned to the MCW Metrobus, with Alexander body, as its last standard double-deck type.

Midland started buying Leyland Nationals in 1978, and Leyland Tigers in 1983.

Early in Midland's existence a number of Northern double-deckers — Daimlers and Leylands — were transferred south, and in 1966 the acquisition of Carmichael (Highland) of Glenboig yielded a mixed bag of 30 Albions and Leylands. The older buses were quickly sold, but five rare ex-Glasgow Corporation Leyland Worldmasters, some L1 Leopards, a Tiger Cub coach, a highbridge PD3 and two Albion Aberdonian coaches lingered for a number of years.

As a consequence of the acquisition of David MacBrayne in 1969 and the decision to split its bus operations between existing SBG companies, Midland received some Bedford VAS1 and VAM5 coaches with Duple bodies to run coach tours from Glasgow.

Transfers from other group fleets in 1975 brought ex-SOL Leopards, ex-Central Fleetlines and ex-Fife Fleetlines into the Midland fleet.

Alexander (Fife) started in 1961 with a fairly mixed fleet. Its oldest buses were Leylands dating back to 1937 and subsequent vehicles were mainly Bristols, Guys and Leylands. The Fife company continued to buy AEC Reliances, Leyland Tiger Cubs and Bristol FLF6Gs (and FS6Gs), but in 1963 received the first of a large fleet of Albion Lowlanders, and in 1964 chose 36ft AEC Reliances for the services to Edinburgh across the new Forth Road Bridge. Thirty-two more Lowlanders appeared in 1965-7, but these were cascaded from the Central and Western fleets. Older double-deckers acquired were 12 early ex-Central Lodekkas.

In 1965 Fife received its first Albion Vikings for less remunerative services, and in 1968 took the only Bristol RELL6L/ECW buses delivered to an SBG company. That year it also took its first Daimler Fleetlines and in 1970 the first of many Leyland Leopard/Alexander Y-types. Like the other

The longer 31ft Bristol/ECW Lodekka was developed partly with SBG's need for high-capacity buses in mind. Alexander (Fife) FRD201 (HXA 401E) at Edinburgh bus station on a Dunfermline service; double-deckers were frequently needed for the Forth Road Bridge services, but could not be used over the bridge in high winds. It is a 1967 FLF6G with 76-seat body, one of 18 bought by Fife that year. Between 1965 and 1967 SBG fleets received 126 long Lodekkas: Central took 83, Eastern 25 and Fife 18; most were 76-seaters, but some of the Central buses were 78-seaters — the equivalent of Atlanteans or Fleetlines. *Gavin Booth*

Older buses inherited by the new Alexander (Northern) company in 1961 included AEC Regals dating back to the early postwar period. Dundee (D) based NA34 (AWG 621), a 1947 AEC Regal O662 with Alexander 35-seat body, is seen in Dundee in Northern days on the route to Inchture. This bus remained in service until 1967. *Harry Hay*

Alexander companies it moved to Fords for its lightweight needs, though Fife's were all Duple-bodied coaches.

Fife received SBG's first Ailsas in 1975, and went on to build up a fleet of 74, all with Alexander bodies. It then moved on to Volvo's underfloor-engined Citybus model; two of its Citybuses had double-deck coach bodies. It also took ten Leyland Olympians in 1983, and in 1983/4 bought a number of former Grampian and Tayside Daimler Fleetlines and Grampian Leyland Atlanteans.

Leyland Nationals were bought in 1978-80 and a small number of Leyland Tigers arrived in 1983/5.

Alexander (Northern) also inherited an elderly fleet, mostly AECs, Albions, Bedfords and Leylands, but quickly invested in new vehicles. At first the AEC Reliance was the standard single-decker, but from 1965 Northern's choice for full-size buses was the Leyland Leopard, with the Albion Viking VK43L for more rural duties. The first new Northern double-deckers were Leyland Titan PD3s, but in 1963 two Albion Lowlanders were bought, after which there was then a 15-year gap until more new double-deckers — Daimler Fleetlines — were bought. In the meantime, older double-deckers were cascaded from other SBG fleets: Albion

Lowlanders and Leyland PD2s and PD3s from Western, two ex-Baxter's AEC Regent Vs from SOL, and Fleetlines from Central and Midland.

Variety came to the Northern fleet following a series of takeovers in the 1960s. From Strachan's Deeside Omnibus Service came short-lived Fodens and a longer-lived AEC Reliance coach. From Simpson's of Rosehearty came AECs, Bedfords, Fords and Leylands; the Bedfords and some of the Fords went to Highland, the newer Fords remained, and some ex-Yorkshire Traction Leyland PS1s rebodied as double-deckers stayed in the fleet for a few years. Burnett's of Mintlaw yielded an all-AEC fleet, including ex-City of Oxford Regals and Regents; longest-lasting were some Reliances. Mitchell of Luthermuir had a more mixed fleet of Bristols, Fords, Leylands and a Guy; the Fords and Tiger Cubs survived into the 1970s.

In the 1980s Northern invested in respectable numbers of new buses. There were Leyland Tiger buses and coaches, Leyland National 2s, 89 Leyland Olympians (including, uniquely for SBG, batches with two doors for Aberdeen city services), single-deck and double-deck MCW Metroliner coaches, plus a few experimental, full-size lightweight single-

Fourteen AECs passed to Northern in 1967 with the business of Burnett of Mintlaw, including this 1955 AEC Reliance MU3RV with 34-seat centre-entrance Harrington body — a rarity in a Scottish fleet. It had been new to another local operator, McIntyre of Bucksburn, passing to Burnett in 1960. It was withdrawn in 1968. *Harry Hay*

Two-door buses were not bought by SBG companies until 1986, when Northern Scottish bought the first of 18 Leyland Olympian ONLXB/1RVs with 73-seat Alexander RL bodies for competitive services in Aberdeen, where Grampian Transport buses had two doors as standard. The Olympians wore a blue/yellow/cream livery and City Bus fleetnames; five of the 1986 delivery are seen before entering service. *Gavin Booth collection*

89

Central bought its first 36ft Leyland Leopards with Alexander Y-type bodywork in 1964 and ordered increasing numbers of these until 1982, by which time more than 400 had joined the fleet. One of the first deliveries, T18 (AGM 618B), a 1964 Leopard PSU3/1R 53-seater, is seen at Balloch, with a lowbridge Leyland PD2/30 in the background, representing the type of bus the early Leopards would replace. *Harry Hay*

deckers which were being considered for the type of work previously handled by Fords. There was a Volvo B57 with Alexander Y-type body (the last Y-type built) and a Dennis Lancet/Y-type, and these were followed by five more Lancets with Alexander's new P-type body.

Central SMT

Central tended to work its vehicles hard, and often replaced them earlier than other group companies — sometimes, one suspected, because they didn't suit the company's operations.

In 1949 Central's oldest buses were Leyland Lions dating back to 1934, and other prewar survivors were Leylands bought new by Central, and curiosities like ex-Baillie AEC and Albion double-deckers. During the war Central had received some 'unfrozen' buses: Leyland TD7s and a solitary Bristol K5G, and Daimler and Guy utility double-deckers.

After the war Central dual-sourced, buying Guys and Leylands. The Guys were Arab II and Arab III double-deckers, as well as Arab III and UF single-deckers. The Leylands were Titan PD1s and PD1As (a type it continued to buy until 1952, when the PD2 was well established elsewhere), and then PD2s. No more Guys were bought after 1954, for in 1955 Central switched to the Bristol LD6G as its Gardner-engined double-decker. The longer Bristol FLF6G was bought from 1963, and Central was one of three SBG companies (the others being Eastern and Fife) to buy the extra-long 31ft Lodekka, which it specified with 78 seats. Central was also the only SBG company to buy the short FSF6G type.

In 1962/3 Central took 30 Albion Lowlanders, but by 1965 had passed these on to the Fife and Highland companies. Apart from the Titans and Lodekkas, it was never comfortable with double-deckers: its Bristol VRTs were included in the big SBG/NBC swap, its 35 Fleetlines were famously dispersed around the group, and nine of its 30 Volvo Ailsas were cascaded to Eastern in 1988. In fact, Central had become very much a single-deck company — a far cry from the double-deck dominance of the early postwar years. Its chosen model was the Leyland Leopard/Alexander Y-type, and its Leopard fleet ultimately numbered 440.

Central's main acquisition was Laurie ('Chieftain') of Hamilton, with 31 buses. These were mostly Leylands, though there was one Guy double-decker and two Bedfords. The Leylands included 16 ex-London RTLs and two Atlanteans, which became the first rear-engined buses to operate for an SBG company. The RTLs survived until 1964-6, and the Atlanteans — perhaps amazingly, given Central's double-deck record — until 1969.

In its later years Central found a double-deck type that it seemed it could live with. The Dennis Dominator was first tried in 1978, and Central went on to build up a fleet of 51. It also took some Dennis Dorchesters, a Gardner underfloor-engined chassis. Central received ten Leyland Olympians and also took Leyland's Tiger in fair numbers — many with Gardner engines, and most with Alexander's TS body (a bus-seated version of the dual-purpose TE). Leyland Nationals were also bought.

90

Leyland's attempt to offer SBG an alternative to the Lodekka was the lowheight Albion Lowlander, and SBG fleets received 194 Lowlanders between 1962 and 1965. They were never as highly regarded as Lodekkas, and some 90 were cascaded to the Fife and Highland fleets, including Central A20 (FGM 20), a 1963 Lowlander LR1 with 72-seat Alexander body, which lasted just two years before it was sold on to Fife. The Alexander bodies were rather more ungainly than those built by Northern Counties. A Glasgow Corporation AEC Regent V/Alexander follows A20 through the Glasgow streets in this 1964 view. *Harry Hay*

Western SMT received the only two Bristol FL-type Lodekkas bought by SBG; these were FL6Gs new in 1961. DB1623 (RAG 389), with 70-seat ECW body, is seen when new at Whitesands, Dumfries, alongside DC334 (BAG 148), a 1947 AEC Regent O662 with 53-seat lowbridge Northern Counties bodywork, and a Roe-bodied Leyland Titan PD1 of Clark of Dumfries. Western acquired the Clark business in 1965. *Gavin Booth*

Western SMT

Western's 1949 fleet included many prewar Leylands — the oldest dating back to 1932 — as well as 'unfrozen' Leylands and utility Daimlers and Guys. Like other SMT group companies, it had Leyland Tigers rebuilt to Titan specification and fitted with new Alexander utility double-deck bodies. After the war Western had bought AECs, Albions, Daimlers, Guys and Leylands, a contrast to the high degree of standardisation before the war.

The 28 buses of Dunlop of Greenock were absorbed into the main fleet in 1949, as were 120 buses from Greenock Motor Services and 25 from Rothesay Motor Services, both of which had operated as subsidiary companies. Then in 1950 came 138 buses with the business of Caledonian Omnibus — AECs, Albions, Dennises and Leylands, as well as some Tilling standard Bristol/ECW L5Gs, K5Gs and K6Bs. The Western fleet grew further with the 22 double-deckers from Paisley & District in 1950, followed a few months later by 109 buses from Young's of Paisley. Many of the Young's buses stayed in the Western fleet for more than a decade — mostly newer Daimler and Leyland double-deckers, always easily identified with their XS registrations.

With this substantial and mixed inheritance, Western set about standardising its growing fleet. In 1951/3 it bought 55 ex-London Transport utility Guy Arabs, and had most of them rebodied by Alexander and Croft. The chassis of a further ten

London Arabs were rebuilt and received new Northern Counties bodies complete with 'new-look' fronts.

After a few years standardising on Guys, Western went for triple-sourcing, buying a mix of Bristols, Guys and Leylands, which allowed the company to concentrate on just two engine types: Gardner and Leyland. Guy Arab single- and double-deckers were bought between 1952 and 1956. Bristol supplied Lodekkas from 1955, followed by LS6Gs in 1957 and MW6Gs in 1958-62; these single-deckers were unique in that they carried Alexander bodies, the only non-ECW LSs and MWs ever built. The Leylands were all double-deckers — PD2s and PD3s — until 1960, when Leopard L1s were bought. From 1963 the 36ft-long Leyland Leopard/Alexander Y-type became the company's standard single-decker.

Western always had a commitment to the Glasgow-London service. In 1951, facing competition from Northern Roadways, it received 14 AEC Regal IV/Alexander coaches that had been intended for SOL, and updated its London fleet regularly over the succeeding years, first with Guy Arab UFs and LUFs and then with Leyland Leopard L1s — the very first Leopards for SBG. Some 36ft Leopards for the London service followed in 1963/4, and then came Bristol RELH6Gs and REMH6Gs, the latter with Alexander M-type bodies; this style of body was fitted to Volvo B58s for Western in 1975.

After years of Leyland PD3s and Bristol Lodekkas, Western turned to the Albion Lowlander (from 1962) and Daimler

92

Fleetline (from 1965) for its double-deck requirements; within a few years many of Western's Lowlanders had been transferred to Fife and Highland. Although it had built up a large quantity of Fleetlines, in 1969/70 Western received Bristol VRTs, most of which went to NBC companies in 1973/4 in exchange for Bristol FLFs.

Although Western took responsibility for MacBrayne's Glasgow-Campbeltown section, it only took four small Bedfords as part of the deal.

Western dual-sourced its single-deck bus requirements from 1975 when it took Seddon Pennine VIIs as well as Leyland Leopards. It bought large batches of Leyland Fleetline double-deckers in 1979/80, and in 1983 turned briefly to the Dennis Dominator for its Gardner-engined double-deck requirements. Other double-deckers were Volvo Ailsas in 1978/80, and in the early 1980s Western bought a number of former London Transport DMS-type Daimler Fleetlines.

Still determined to get Gardner-engined chassis, Western took Dennis Dorchesters and Gardner-engined Leyland Tigers in the 1980s. Western's front-line coach fleet was mainly composed of Volvo B10Ms with Berkhof, Duple and Plaxton bodies, and there were MCW Metroliner double-deck coaches. Other unusual purchases were Duple 425 integral coaches, and

Van Hool integral coaches that came from the fleet of Newton of Dingwall.

Highland Omnibuses

When Highland was set up in 1952, it started with 69 vehicles from the Highland Transport company as its base fleet. These were older AECs, Albions, Bedfords and Leylands, with one TSM, and a substantial post-1944 fleet of single- and double-deck Guys. At the same time, the smaller (27-vehicle) fleet of Macrae & Dick was incorporated, consisting mainly of Albions, Austins and Bedfords, and there were 24 buses from Alexanders' Inverness area.

Highland received its first 'new' buses in 1952: six Guy Arab single-deckers with SOL bodies, rebuilt from London double-deckers; another 12 similar buses followed in 1953/4. At the same time, Highland was receiving the first of a continuing stream of cascaded buses from other Scottish group companies. The first all-new buses were AEC Monocoaches and Reliances delivered in 1957, and small batches of Reliances, often similar to contemporary SOL deliveries, followed until 1962.

Most cascaded buses were fairly elderly, as many were used for transporting construction workers to and from the site of

Western contrasts — three vehicles lined up in 1983. On the left is the prototype MCW Metroliner (registration TSX 1Y), still owned by MCW at that time; beside it is 1983 Volvo B10M/Duple Goldliner III 46-seater V151 (TSD 151Y), in blue/white Scottish livery for London services. On the right is VA 5777, the 1926 AEC 413 with 29-seat Metcalfe body that started life with the Glasgow General company, and found its way into Western ownership via the Sword Collection; in the 1970s it was restored and repainted in red/cream livery as a Midland Bus Services vehicle.
Gavin Booth collection

Probably the most distinctive vehicle to join the new Highland Omnibuses fleet in 1952 from Highland Transport was this 1951 Guy Arab III with full-fronted Strachans 57-seat lowbridge bodywork, complete with platform doors. E72 (EST 392) remained in the Highland fleet until 1970. It is seen at Highland's Carse Road depot in Inverness (I).
Gavin Booth collection

Highland started what became a fleet of over 180 Fords with four Thames 570E models transferred from Scottish Omnibuses following the acquisition of Stark's of Dunbar. T4 (GSS 452), with Duple (Northern) Yeoman bodywork, had been new to Stark's in 1963, and is seen in fawn livery at Inverness Airport in 1965.
Gavin Booth

▶ the Dounreay nuclear plant near Thurso, but SOL transferred 12 seven-year-old Lodekkas in 1963 for Inverness town services, which were followed by Albion Lowlanders from Central and Western.

Between 1964 and 1977 only Bedford and, increasingly, Ford buses and coaches were bought new by Highland, except for four Leyland Leopards in 1973. Then, in 1978/9, it received its first-ever new double-deckers, when 15 new Leyland Fleetlines with ECW bodies were bought, and in 1980/1 there were 18 Leyland National 2s.

In the 1980s Highland received Duple-bodied Leyland Tiger coaches, Alexander-bodied Leyland Olympian double-deckers and, as had happened throughout its history, various cast-offs from other SBG fleets.

Highland assumed responsibility for the majority of the former David MacBrayne bus services, and between 1970 and 1972 a total of 115 ex-MacBrayne buses and coaches passed to Highland. These were AEC Reliances and Bedford C5Z1s, SBs

and VAS1s with Duple group or Plaxton bodies. From 1970 Highland abandoned its dark red/cream livery in favour of a striking poppy red/peacock blue scheme, which was said to reflect the MacBrayne influence.

94

6. The SBG Legacy

For nearly 60 years SMT and SBG played a significant part in Scottish life, moving more than two million passengers every working day at one stage, and employing tens of thousands of people around the country.

The group always did things its own way, and tended to resent interference from outside. The majority of its managers worked their way up from within the group, and job vacancies were normally only advertised internally. This produced a breed of manager who had been brought up in the group's ways, and contributed to the group's efficiency and profitability. Occasionally an 'outsider' would join the group — notably Moris Little as its Chairman in 1963 — and there were other directors who came from the municipal sector in Scotland. Most of the Planning & Development Officers came from outside the group (and in some cases outside the bus industry), and brought a fresh approach to the business of running buses.

SBG was noted for its conservative approach to bus-buying. It looked for rugged, economical and reliable buses, with the maximum seating capacity, and these provided straightforward, no-frills transport. It instinctively held back from types like the Leyland National until vehicle shortages forced its hand, although the National went on to become a useful urban tool. The Leyland Leopard with 53-seat Alexander Y-type bus body is probably the type most people will automatically associate with SBG, and this (together with the Seddon Pennine VII)

was certainly the group's workhorse.

Nevertheless, SBG could surprise. Its support for the Volvo Ailsa and its involvement in the design of the MCW Metroliner double-deck coach were two good examples. And its M-type body for Scotland-London services, developed with Alexander Coachbuilders, was ahead of its time with its high build and small double-glazed windows; the group's London coaches since the 1930s had featured toilet accommodation and 'proper' reclining seats.

Deregulation led to SBG companies pulling out of the more rural services they had developed, a concentration on the long trunk routes that so characterised SMT and SBG over the years, and a greater involvement in urban services. There are still many services, run by the privatised companies that succeeded SBG, that are relatively unchanged after half a century, but many more that have been changed to reflect the reality of Scotland in the 21st century. And there are still SBG-ordered buses in service in considerable numbers, though their numbers drop every time new vehicles take the road.

Good financial housekeeping and a shrewd, down-to-earth approach to bus operation are two of the main legacies of SBG. The Alexanders, Dicks and Swords in the 1920s and 1930s did a lot to lay the foundations of an industry that is still recognisable today, and generations of SBG staff carried their vision forward.

Further Reading

The Scottish Bus Group, its companies and its predecessors have not been well covered in print. There are mainly pictorial books on Alexanders (published by Allan T. Condie), Neil MacDonald's *The Western Way* (TPC, 1983), and D. L. G. Hunter's *From SMT to Eastern Scottish* (John Donald, 1987). Although the Western and Eastern books are out of print, they may be available through specialist dealers.

For reference I used BTC, THC and STG annual reports and the Fleet Histories published by the PSV Circle and the Omnibus Society.

This book can only give a flavour of SBG, but a detailed history of the group is in preparation.